QUIET LEADERSHIP

CARLO ANCELOTTI

QUIET LEADERSHIP

Winning hearts, minds and matches

WITH CHRIS BRADY
AND MIKE FORDE

PORTFOLIO
PENGUIN

PORTFOLIO PENGUIN

UK | USA | Canada | Ireland | Australia
India | New Zealand | South Africa

Portfolio Penguin is part of the Penguin Random House group of companies
whose addresses can be found at global.penguinrandomhouse.com.

First published 2016

001

Copyright © Axiomatix Ltd, 2016

The moral right of the author has been asserted

Set in 13.75/16.5 pt Garamond MT Std
Typeset by Jouve (UK), Milton Keynes
Printed in Great Britain by Clays Ltd, St Ives plc

A CIP catalogue record for this book is available from the British Library

HARDBACK ISBN: 978–0–241–25878–1
TRADE PAPERBACK ISBN: 978–0–241–24493–7

www.greenpenguin.co.uk

Giuseppe and Carlo Ancelotti, Stadio Comunale, Turin 1985

Carlo Ancelotti
In loving memory of my first great leader, my father, Giuseppe

Chris Brady
For my wife, Anita, and my favourite daughter,
Eleanor, because I love them both

Mike Forde
To my father who taught me the responsibility that goes with
leading others; to my mother who showed me how to
create an environment for people to be inspired and comfortable
to be themselves and to my wife, Daniela, who unconditionally
supports me daily to be the best version of me I can be.

CONTENTS

Preface

As a young boy growing up on a farm in the north of Italy, did I ever imagine myself becoming a leader in a multimillion-pound global industry? Of course not. All I wanted to do was play football.

Now, when I look back, I can see that we were poor but happy and my family taught me the beginnings of many of the lessons you will read about over the course of this book. Things like respect and loyalty, the value of money and hard work, the importance of family – these seeds were planted early for me, and they grew and flowered when I was privileged to embark on a career first as a professional football player and then as a manager.

Quiet Leadership is a collection of reflections on my time in football and my thoughts and philosophies on what it takes to be a leader in my profession. By extension, these lessons can be taken into other professions; there are similarities between leaders in all fields, be it in football or business, and I am a big believer in importing knowledge from other areas, just as I have exported my own expertise to Paris, London, Madrid and now Munich. We should never cease to learn.

A 'quiet' approach to leadership might sound soft or perhaps even weak to some, but that is not what it means to me, and it is definitely not what it means to anyone who has ever played with me or for me. The kind of quiet I am talking about is a strength. There is power and authority in being calm and measured, in building trust and making decisions coolly, in using influence and persuasion and in being professional in your approach. When you watch Vito Corleone in *The Godfather*, do you see a weak, quiet man or do you see a calm, powerful man in charge of his situation?

My approach is born of the idea that a leader should not need to rant or rave or rule with an iron fist, but rather that their power should be implicit. It should be crystal clear who is in charge, and their authority must result from respect and trust rather than fear. I believe that I have earned the respect I am shown, partly through a successful career delivering trophies for my clubs, but perhaps more importantly because of the fact that I respect those I work with. These people trust me to do the right thing, just as I trust them with their roles in the organization.

My method of leading is part of who I am – it is true to my character and an essential element of my personality. Leadership can be learned but cannot be imitated. It is possible to observe other great leaders at work, but if your natural inclination is to be quiet, calm and take care of others it is unwise to try to be anyone else.

The 'Quiet Way' has been with me from my childhood with my father and in football ever since I became captain of Roma as a player, continuing when I joined Milan, where the players looked to me as one of the leaders in the dressing room, and then throughout my time managing not only that club but also teams including Chelsea, Paris Saint-Germain and Real Madrid. It is the same approach that I am taking with me to Bayern Munich as I begin a new challenge there, and it is the very approach that anyone hiring me knows they are buying into.

When I left Madrid in May 2015, I decided that this would be a perfect time both to sort out a long-standing neck problem that had been restricting me more and more and to take a sabbatical. I was able to spend more time with my wife, Mariann – we'd married the previous year, shortly after Madrid won the Champions League – at our home in Vancouver. Then I waited to see which jobs were vacant for the next season, because I definitely wanted to work again. After playing, it is the best job in the world, to manage a football club, and I have been so lucky to manage the champion teams in some of Europe's greatest cities.

I knew that there would be pressure at different stages of my sabbatical for me to start at a new club, whenever other managers in Europe looked to be coming to the end of their own periods in charge. I was linked with Liverpool FC in the media – a great honour – and I was definitely interested, but not disappointed when I wasn't appointed. Jürgen Klopp is right for them; he will succeed there. My rest away from the game has been good for me too, but when an opportunity as great as the Bayern Munich job comes along, it's impossible to refuse. I am planning to have the longest period of sustained success of my career.

What you won't find in this book is a chapter on relationships. This is because relationships form the foundation of everything I do as a leader, so they feature on every page: relationships with those above me, with my support team and, most importantly, with the players.

Without the players there can be no game, just as without people and a product, there is no business. The thousands in the stadiums, the millions watching at home – they're not paying to see me, or Pep Guardiola or Sir Alex Ferguson on the sidelines; they want to see the players, the magic they can conjure up. Working with these athletes, taking care of them and helping them develop and grow, building trust and loyalty, sharing our successes and bouncing back together from disappointment, this is the heart of my job for me. This is why I get up for work every day with a smile on my face.

As children, we first play the game because we fall in love with it. When I started playing professionally, I couldn't believe my luck at being paid to do something I love. Sometimes, somewhere along the way the pressures and difficulties on and off the pitch can cause the passion to fade or die. It is my responsibility to help the players stay in love. If I can succeed in this, then I am happy.

Working on this book, sharing stories and many great

memories – as well as some difficult ones – with my two co-writers and friends, Chris Brady and Mike Forde, has been a very rewarding experience for me. My hope is that you will find something in here to take into your own life and career – and perhaps something that makes you happy too.

Carlo Ancelotti
February 2016

INTRODUCTION

CHRIS BRADY

This book took several years to pull together, mostly because the three of us – Carlo Ancelotti, Mike Forde and I – wanted it to be a genuinely collaborative piece of work. We started out by defining what we *didn't* want the book to become. It wouldn't be a standard autobiography, it wouldn't be aimed primarily at a football audience, it wouldn't be an academic business book and it certainly wouldn't be a kiss-and-tell.

We agreed we wanted it to be a book of which we could all be proud. A book that would appeal to a business and a sports audience either involved in, fascinated by or aspiring to leadership roles in the broadest sense. We wanted it to be honest, original, compelling and worthy of discussion and dissent by a curious readership. It isn't a series of stories, though, of course, they are important; instead it is a book based primarily on the reflections of an expert practitioner in leading talented teams in one of the most competitive markets imaginable.

We have set out to reveal Carlo Ancelotti's fundamental

principles and leadership journey, his core business and skills, his formative experiences, how he learned to lead, and the Ancelotti brand – how he sees himself and is perceived by others. We are aiming to get to the heart of how he's continually developed, dealt with setbacks and delivered repeatedly on the biggest possible stage.

With our business and sports leadership backgrounds, we have used this opportunity to hold up the generic theories of experts and academics to intense scrutiny, comparing them unflinchingly to Ancelotti's direct experience. As the professional landscape changes radically across all sectors and markets, business leaders have to be better armed to deal with managing diverse and highly talented – and often problematic – workforces. Using the backdrop of elite sport, we will draw out the leadership insights and lessons of one of the greatest talent managers in the world. We will investigate and challenge strongly held beliefs around how you should lead and manage the best people around you.

Naturally, the central voice is Carlo's, as is the grammar. The narrative of the book is told directly by him – the result of more than fifty hours of in-depth interviews we conducted with him around the world, focusing on how his experiences illuminated critical business issues both current and timeless. The lessons are implicit in his reflections, but for ease of reference we have included summaries at the end of each chapter explaining the main points of the 'Quiet Way'.

We wanted this to be a book simultaneously *by* Ancelotti and *about* Ancelotti, so we have also included interviews with those who know his leadership qualities best. You know what they say: if you really want to know who you are, you have to learn what people say about you when you leave the room. We asked Carlo's teammates, colleagues, opponents and, perhaps most importantly, those who have played for him to talk about him behind his back. Players interviewed include Cristiano Ronaldo, David Beckham, Zlatan Ibrahimović and John Terry, all of whom have also played for other giants of football management, the likes of Pep Guardiola, José Mourinho and Sir Alex Ferguson. Ferguson also features as an opponent and his colleagues include Adriano Galliani, the CEO of AC Milan, who, in one role or another, was Ancelotti's boss for around thirteen years when Ancelotti was either a player or a coach.

It is testament to the strength of the bonds that Ancelotti makes, and the impact he has had on these elite names, that they all freely gave their time to talk about him. Indeed, they were so keen and so lyrical and passionate once they got started, that the interviews almost always overran their slots – I think

Zlatan would still be talking now if, after ninety minutes, I hadn't tentatively prompted him to wrap things up.

*

Why is there a need for yet another book on 'leadership'? It must be the most discussed and written-about topic in management. Blogs, TED talks, books, the media, academic articles . . . it's everywhere, and you can't get away from it. Historically, there have been more theories of leadership than you can shake a big stick at. Early theorists even assumed that leadership was directly related to membership of the aristocracy and was, therefore, genetically preordained. This led to the 'great man' theory of leadership, which is still prevalent today and includes such diverse luminaries as Moses, the Dalai Lama, Patton, Crazy Horse, Custer, Martin Luther King, Nelson Mandela, Elizabeth I, Florence Nightingale, Colin Powell and Genghis Khan – take your pick or name your own.

Other pivotal ideas have included the trait theory of leadership, which argues that there are certain generic traits which can be identified in all great leaders. By contrast, situational theorists argued that great leaders emerged as a result of place, circumstance and time, or what we lay people might call luck – the place where preparation meets opportunity. Others were more interested in the development of the individual within an organization; for example the American psychologist Abraham Maslow emphasized the manager's role in supporting subordinates.

High on the current buzz list are authentic leadership, which entails ethical and transparent behaviour; transformational leadership, where leaders forgo self-interest by transforming and inspiring followers to perform beyond expectations; and servant leadership, which extends Robert Greenleaf's original 1970s work in which leadership was framed as focusing on the needs of the followers (employees, players) and where the leaders' primary motivation is to serve. Greenleaf prioritized the 'caring' nature of these leaders, not in an altruistic way but as a managerial imperative.

As Pat Summitt, one of the greatest if lesser known coaches in sporting history, has said, 'People don't care how much you know until they know how much you care. To get people to work hard for you, you need to show them you want them to achieve career success for *their* sake.' There are clear echoes of Jim Collins's 'Level 5' leaders who, Collins argues in his classic *Good to Great*, possess the paradoxical mix of ambition and humility. These leaders are highly ambitious, but the focus of their ambition is not themselves; it is on those who will deliver success (employees or players), and they also feel no need to inflate their own egos.

It is estimated that as much as $50 billion is spent annually on leadership training and development around the world. Perhaps that's because trust in the qualities of those in corporate, political and military leadership positions is at such a low ebb that we are trying to rectify the situation in some sense. It's also an indicator of how important the issue is perceived to be.

However, perhaps the real reason we find it so difficult to settle on a specific leadership model is because each leader is, in fact, an amalgam of all the various traits, styles, characteristics and approaches mentioned above, but with the ingredients mixed in different proportions.

If so, then Carlo Ancelotti's understated leadership style, his 'quiet leadership', may be unique to him and to the experiences that have shaped him during a life spent almost entirely in the goldfish bowl of professional football in countries such as Italy, Spain and England – and now Germany. Countries where the sheer interest in the sport and the consequent financial implications are at their most intense. Unique or not, it is clearly an effective and successful approach and one which demands our attention, not least because, as will become clear, Ancelotti ticks a huge number of the boxes identified in any current leadership debate.

*

Of all the leadership challenges, one of the most difficult is managing talent. Most research shows that it is highest on the list of concerns for CEOs. Management guru Tom Peters has asked:

> Are you a certified talent fanatic? Whether you're the head of a six-person project team or the CEO . . . you must become as obsessed about finding and developing top-flight people as the general manager of any professional sports franchise is about recruiting and training top-flight players. In an age when value added flows from creativity, a quirky, energetic, engaged talent pool has become the primary basis of competitive advantage.*

What better field, then, to study than football, where the coverage and interest in the management of talent is almost an entertainment industry in itself? The so-called 'war for talent'

* Tom Peters, 'Leaders As Talent Fanatics', *Leadership Excellence Essentials* 23, 11 (2006), p. 12.

has been a staple factor in football since it was first played, certainly since its first professional incarnation. Football clubs pay out, on average, more than 50 per cent of their revenue on less than 10 per cent of their employees.

The most recent Deloitte Millennial Survey, conducted across twenty-nine industrialized countries (in all of which football is played professionally), found that millennials want more open, collaborative, flexible working environments; they are imaginative, think laterally and believe that they can do anything. They are less loyal because they now recognize that employers treat them as assets and consequently they're going to treat their employers similarly. Deloitte concludes that 'millennials have forced us to rethink the way we work'. Well, virtually every elite footballer is a millennial. So, again, what better laboratory is there than football in which to observe and analyse the people who lead this type of workforce? Equally, the way Ancelotti manages upwards is similarly instructive for anyone in modern business.

The book is called *Quiet Leadership* for a reason; Ancelotti goes about his business in a calm but authoritative way that can go under the radar of a media desperate for scandal. When managing the super egos of the world's greatest players he has been described as the 'diva whisperer'. When managing upwards, Ancelotti is described as the uber-diplomat; Italian journalist Gabriele Marcotti has spoken of Ancelotti's 'biblical patience' with the notoriously demanding Real Madrid president, Florentino Pérez. Indeed, when he appointed Ancelotti, Pérez described him as a manager who could keep the stars happy while finding a way to make it work without grumbling in public. What more could a president want?*

When Ancelotti was at Chelsea there was a rocky period. His management was coming under scrutiny from the media as a result of some leaked briefings from within the club. After he held a press conference, *Guardian* journalist Barney Ronay wrote a revealingly accurate description of Ancelotti's 'Quiet Way':

> What today provided was a welcome draught of Ancelotti's own wonderfully moreish charm. For the neutral, he has been a disarming presence at the heart of the Chelsea project, maintaining throughout his early successes an air of something jarringly wry and sceptical within the corporate labyrinth of the club's managerial superstructure. Admittedly, this is almost entirely down to his rogue eyebrow, that arching salt and pepper caterpillar,

---

* Clearly much more, because less than two years later Pérez sacked Ancelotti and only a few months afterwards his successor, Rafa Benítez, had also gone.

perpetually humpbacked with what appears to be a sense of portable deadpan irony. The Ancelotti eyebrow seems to speak to us directly, offering its own subtitled counter-commentary on whatever conciliatory patter might be emerging from the Ancelotti mouth. It is a quality the English have warmed to. We understand eyebrow speak. The unspoken, the taciturn and the repressed: this kind of talk is our kind of talk.

(*Guardian*, 22 November 2010)

We couldn't have put it better ourselves.

PART ONE
The Leadership Arc

CHRIS BRADY

There is an extensive literature around the concept of what we will call, in this book, the leadership arc. Whether it is the mid-2000s work of Ken Blanchard or George D. Parsons and Richard T. Pascale's 'Summit Syndrome',* or even workshops taking place at the Wharton School, there is widespread recognition that the careers of even the greatest leaders follow a similar pattern.

Currently the average tenure of a FTSE 100 CEO is 5.18 years; for English Premier League managers it's just 2.36 years (if Arsène Wenger is excluded from that equation, the average drops to 1.7 years). In Italy's Serie A the average is 1.31 years; in Spain's La Liga it's 1.34 years. The longevity record is barely better in other sports. In the USA, a manager in the NFL (National Football League) has an average tenure of 3.4 seasons; a new

---

*George D. Parsons and Richard T. Pascale, 'Crisis at the Summit', *Harvard Business Review*, March 2007.

manager in the NBA (National Basketball Association) can expect 2.4 seasons.

The end can often be sudden and brutal. The English professional leagues saw a total of forty-seven managerial dismissals in the 2014–15 season, and seventeen of those were first-time managers, many of whom will find it very difficult to get another opportunity to manage.* Furthermore, more than 150 coaches lost their jobs as a direct consequence of the instability caused by sacking the manager and the desire of the club to bring in a host of new staff. Other than for an elite few, reference to the merry-go-round of football management is far from reality; in the majority of cases their family has suddenly lost its main source of income. This is not a business for the faint hearted.

The parallels with business are very clear. Every week a sporting manager is subjected to the same scrutiny that a CEO receives with quarterly statements. As an English Premier League chairman once stated, 'Every week 40,000 stakeholders turn up and tell me how they think I'm running the business.' Everything in sport is compressed into the span of a single

* Statistics from the League Managers Association.

season, whereas the life cycle in business, before results can be validated, is likely to be around ten quarters or thirty months.

For both business and sport there seems to be an inexorable arc to the leadership lifespan in successful organizations, notwithstanding outliers such as Sir Alex Ferguson, Bill Belichick at the New England Patriots or Gregg Popovich at the San Antonio Spurs.

Is such an arc inevitable, or is it possible to identify key tipping points, moments at which the leaders themselves can alter the course of events either by exiting of their own accord or by remaining in the post by changing the dynamic? Carlo Ancelotti's career and successes in four of the top European leagues suggests both are possible, but require an early awareness of the typical leadership trajectory and an ability to manoeuvre around the pitfalls in each type of trajectory. Now, over to Carlo.

1. Experience

Unless you happen to be a one-off like Sir Alex Ferguson at Manchester United, the careers of leaders in most walks of life follow a similar path. My time at Real Madrid demonstrates it clearly and it shares important similarities with the time I spent at all my clubs.

First, comes the courtship, when the club identifies you and tries to acquire your services. Then comes the honeymoon period, when everyone – the players, the staff, the fans – give you the time to establish yourself, but which unfortunately, as always in life, never lasts long. Next comes success and stability, should you be able to achieve it – for a top club this means trophies, but success is measured differently further down the league. Eventually, this stability plateaus and then the problems begin: the cracks in the relationship. If we look at Madrid, this was undoubtedly when my challenges took hold. Finally, comes the breakup – the inevitable parting of ways. We can call this process, this rise and fall, the leadership arc.

At Madrid, my leadership arc was very tight, very compressed, but it is the same at every top club. It was less than a year for David Moyes at Manchester United. I have had a much shallower arc too, eight years at Milan, which is a very long time to spend at such a big club. The average tenure of a manager in any of the top divisions in England, Spain or Italy is a long way below this: the compressed arc is the norm.

Along the way there are pivotal moments, where the leader can influence events and determine their path, but these key points on the arc have followed me throughout my time in football, starting with my first job.

Climbing the Ladder

First Job: Reggiana

If I were advising the Reggiana president today, when he was contemplating hiring a retired player with local roots to manage the club, I would say: 'What do you want him for? He's got no licence and he's never coached anywhere before. He might have been a good player, but who cares?' Thankfully for me, the crazy way of football does not work like that.

Make no mistake: Reggiana hired me because I was a famous player and a local boy. It's the little things, sometimes. It might not make any sense at all reading it, but

Reggiana made perfect sense for me and vice versa. They had just been relegated to the second division and they needed a name. I had that name and I was ready for it. Not for the project, necessarily, but certainly to be the boss.

Today, I've seen enough to know that you must never think that being a player is enough to be a manager. It enables you to have a relationship with the players and to understand what they need, but the other aspects of management have to be studied and learned. For a good part of my first season at Reggiana I didn't even have a coaching licence. I had completed two elements of it and I would work on the final section while doing the job. I am a strong believer in acquiring your qualifications before starting out on a career, but sometimes it's not possible. There should be no MBA or manager debate. There's no need to choose – both are good.

Since I didn't have my own licence, I needed to employ someone who did to be my assistant and I also needed a goalkeeping coach. I searched the Italian coaching association book for someone who satisfied both criteria. The first name I came to in the alphabetical listings who was suitable and who lived close to Reggiana was Giorgio Ciaschini. I didn't know him, but I called him anyway and he agreed to come and work with me. We stayed together for more than ten years. He became a loyal part of my football family from the start of my time as a manager and, as will become clear throughout this book, loyalty is very important to me.

With a brief from the president at the start of the season that our objective was to win the championship, we were lying at the bottom of the table after seven games. It was probably my fault, through my inexperience, as in the beginning it was not so easy to suddenly be the boss straight from being a player.

Of course, I wasn't totally green. Just before I finished as a player at Milan I was offered the opportunity to be assistant manager to Arrigo Sacchi in the Italian national team. I could have continued to play, but I preferred to stop because I thought the experience with Sacchi would be good for me. That period was critical for me to grow as a manager and maybe without those years with *Gli Azzurri* I would have failed at Reggiana. When I went to Sacchi to tell him that I wanted to take the job at Reggiana and start alone, he said that he thought it was time and wished me good luck. However, even though I had been number two with Sacchi, it is totally different when you are the boss.

The problem is that when you become a manager after finishing a playing career so recently, you think that you know everything. In reality you know nothing. Firstly, there is a difficult and important thing to get right – to have a good relationship with the players but also be the boss at the same time. It is not impossible to do and it is strange that many people think the manager cannot have a strong, positive relationship with the players while still maintaining his authority.

The thing that scared me most, however, was having to put my face in front of the players and speak to them regularly. If the players have a lot of respect of you, you have to speak both *for* them and *with* them. They expect it to be perfect because you are the boss, but it is new to you. You are not used to being in this position, where you have the careers of others in your hands. Understanding and accepting that I was the boss was very difficult for me. I knew my own inadequacies, my own vulnerabilities, and I could not believe that others could not see that. Maybe that's the most difficult element of the transition from worker to boss for most of us.

When it came to speaking in front of the squad and staff, which could be twenty-five, thirty people, they were not all totally attentive and alert. One might be yawning, another could be 'resting their eyes' in the corner, while someone might be staring blankly out the window – someone might even be fast asleep. It's really difficult, at the start, to command everyone's attention all the time.

When I would start the meetings, everyone would usually be listening, but the problems came when I named the team. You have eighteen, maybe twenty players, but once you've named the eleven in the team, the faces of the others, which were so excited before, suddenly become sullen. I knew this because until recently I had been one of them. So for a period when I started, I would leave the naming of the eleven until the end, just before we left the dressing room, to try to keep everyone involved in the proceedings. But no matter when you name the team, you will still always have players who are not happy.

Another difficulty in your first job as the boss is simply how to prepare for the game. Players don't fully appreciate the amount of preparation needed to manage well – I know that I didn't when I was playing. I read that Bill Parcells, the legendary American football head coach, believed that 'everybody has the will to win but only the best have the will to prepare to win'. He was so right. It all looks easy from the dressing room. At the beginning, I didn't even have the answer to questions as simple and fundamental as: 'How are you going to do the training?' I don't know about other first-time managers, so I can't speak for them, but my lack of qualifications at the time meant I didn't have the technical knowledge of how to organize the training properly. I did, however, have my experience with Sacchi to fall back on. In the beginning I just copied his methods, but gradually I began to develop my own ideas and objectives – and my own training schedules.

Giorgio Ciaschini, my assistant, was a massive help for me during this period. I had to learn to speak to the players and for them to believe in me because we needed to start winning. I brought the players together and said to them, 'I have my beliefs about how we should play and behave. If you agree with them, we can stay together. If you don't agree, I don't want to wait for the owner to sack me. I will go now. If we're not together, we can finish here and now.' Almost all of the players were with me. Only two would not follow but, as I've said, you will always have some who are not happy. Gradually, we began to get better results and we finished in the promotion positions. We would play in Serie A the following season.

During those first seven games I thought that I would not make it as a coach. I was worried that maybe this wasn't the right profession for me. There was too much pressure. Most of this pressure, I was putting on myself, as it was at the beginning of my career and I knew how important this first job was if I was going to be successful. Now, I am a member of the League Managers Association, and when I see their research about the time in a job most new managers get, it scares me. I'm glad I didn't know these numbers when I was at Reggiana.

The end of my arc at Reggiana, the breakup, came about not as a sacking, as happened at Real, but because I was offered the job at a bigger club – Parma. The end of an arc can be instigated by the leader, just as it can by the organization, and it is important to be philosophical about the manner of the arc ending. Sometimes you leave on your own terms, sometimes you don't. That's football, just as it is in business.

Second Job: Parma

Parma wanted me because Fabio Capello, who had signed a contract with them, refused to go because he decided to go to Real Madrid. As he had pulled out at the end of the season, they didn't have a lot of time to replace him. I had done well at Reggiana, I knew the general manager of Parma and it was a good move for me, to a bigger club. A new leadership arc began.

Just as at Reggiana, at the beginning the team were not playing well, but in the end we were able to have a successful first season. I had a good squad, with the likes of goalkeeper Gigi Buffon and defender Lilian Thuram, who formed a central defensive partnership with Fabio Cannavaro. They were young, too. Buffon was only seventeen, Thuram around twenty-one and Cannavaro twenty-two or twenty-three. Then I had a striker, Hernán Crespo, whom I had scouted from the Argentinian Olympic team – he was their top scorer in the Olympic Games and only twenty-one years old. In that period we also bought Rivaldo and after that Cafu, although they were immediately loaned to Deportivo de La Coruña and Roma. Parma was a small club then so we had to release players. Maybe Capello had been right after all. Parma had an interesting relationship with the Brazilian side Palmeiras, which worked well for us. Issues such as third-party ownership were not considered important at the time and many of the big European clubs had 'relationships' or 'arrangements' with Latin American counterparts, whereby all sorts of deals could be done.

I finished two seasons at Parma, qualifying for the Champions League and the UEFA Cup, before my first experience of being sacked, after a run of poor results.

After a brief flirtation with Turkish team Fenerbahçe – a case of approaching the leadership arc but not quite embarking upon it – I got lucky. I had been out of work for six months and the Istanbul side were courting me just as Juventus came calling with an alternative, and that made the decision easy for me.

Company Man: Juventus

My courtship with Juventus was a new experience for me. I was about to leave for Turkey to discuss terms with Fenerbahçe when I got a call from Luciano Moggi, the general director of Juventus. He asked me not to commit to anything until I'd met with him, so I went to see him at the home of Antonio Giraudo, the club's technical director. When I arrived I found Giraudo, Moggi and Roberto Bettega, the legendary former Juventus striker, waiting for me. They made their position clear when they simply said: 'We want you to be the next manager of Juve.' They knew my contract at Parma still had time to run – technically, I was on gardening leave – so they accepted that I would have to stay out for one season, but I would be the manager for the 1999–2000 season. A few hours later, I had signed a precontract. As it happened, the incumbent at the time, Marcello Lippi, left Juve early. He hadn't done a good job and he was sacked in January, so I went to Juventus in February 1999, with the club handling the outstanding contractual details.

Juventus was tough for me because, after working at a club like Parma, which was a family, Juventus was like working at a company. Juventus is a great company, a great organization, but for me, going to the training ground was like going to work at a factory. There were impressive people working there – the owner was Gianni Agnelli, there was Luciano Moggi, plus the financial director – but it was not a family, not like Reggiana or Parma or, as I would discover later, Milan. Having achieved some success at Reggiana and Parma I wanted to go to the next level, and by this time I had the confidence to go to a club like Juventus, a club with great tradition and a big history.

Aside from the cultural shift, from the family to a company environment, there was another reason why it was difficult for me in this job: the Juventus supporters hated me. Why? Because I was Roma player, a Milan player. When I was at Parma we had fought against Juventus for the title, so they really hated me. Most of the time I would find them outside the training ground, waiting to bait me. It's true – in Italy this kind of thing happens. It was a big task to win over the fans.

I stayed at Juventus for over two years until they sacked me too, and I stayed out of the game for another four months. The leadership arc at Juventus had been completed before I was ready. In truth it was possibly one that I shouldn't have even started on, but it gave me a taste of what it would be like at a big club, which was where I wanted to manage.

Coming Home

AC Milan

For a long time it looked like I would be heading back to Parma and the relative security of my home region. However, what might have been a backward step was averted by a last-minute phone call from the club that had given me my greatest moments as a player, AC Milan. Milan had just lost 1–0 at Torino and, as it turned out, I was in the mind of Milan's general director Adriano Galliani. He had spoken to me a few days earlier about other matters and while we were talking I had let slip that I would be signing for Parma again.

After the game against Torino, Galliani spoke with Silvio Berlusconi, the owner, and they decided to change coach, immediately focusing on me as their preferred replacement and obviously hoping that I hadn't already signed with Parma. This particular courtship would have to be speedy. Galliani quickly called me and I told him that I was going to sign for Parma the next day.

It was on Monday, when I was on my way to sign a contract with the officials in Parma, that Galliani called me. I had a deal with Parma in place and, only three days before, I had shaken the hand of the club president, Calisto Tanzi.

'Did you sign a contract with Parma?' Galliani asked.

'No, not yet, but I'm on my way now,' I said.

'I'm going to your house,' said Galliani.

'What for?'

'I spoke with Berlusconi and we agree that you have to come here, to Milan. We are ready for you.' And so I switched off my telephone.

Naturally, as soon as I signed the contract for Milan I switched the telephone back on. I needed it to call Tanzi at Parma. I told him, 'Sorry, but Milan is my family. I played there and I am so sorry for this – I hope that you can understand,' and he said to me, 'I understand everything.' Even after fifteen years I'm still not sure if Tanzi was serious. He was indeed the big boss: he was the founder and major shareholder of the Parmalat corporation, which almost wholly owned Parma FC, and he was later indicted and convicted for one of Europe's largest bankruptcies. I had to be pragmatic. Loyalty and integrity have limits; how loyal would Parma have been to me if the season started badly? And Milan was family, which must always be the first loyalty.

I arrived in Milan in November 2001 and it immediately felt like I was home. The team was another matter, however, as it was not so good. Coming home isn't always easy and the first six months were tough. In the transfer market we managed to get Clarence Seedorf and Alessandro Nesta, outstanding players. Nesta was twenty-seven, in his prime, and he cost a lot of money. Initially, the general director was not able to convince Berlusconi to pay such an amount for the player as Berlusconi had some financial problems with his company. He didn't want to risk the judgement of public opinion and be seen to be overspending – especially not for a player like Nesta, a *defender*. Nesta was going to cost €30 million, but even at that price I knew I had to convince Berlusconi that he was vital for us. The constraints on running an organization are not always on public view and, while managers work under the gaze of the public, that gaze cannot always penetrate to see the real reasons for certain actions.

I considered Nesta so vital to the team that I decided to try with Berlusconi myself. He was in Denmark at the time and I told him, 'President, everyone wants to win the Champions League, but if you don't buy Nesta, we won't win it. Give me Nesta and I will give you the Champions League.' In the end it was a great deal for both of us. He bought Nesta and I gave him the Champions League. Later, we would deliver another Champions League and another final, semi-final, quarter-final – it was a fantastic period for the club.

My leadership arc at Milan was the longest of my career so far – eight years – and the length of my tenure gave me the opportunity to change the players over time, to gradually transform the team in my own vision. The biggest changes came at the beginning, as a matter of necessity because the squad was not good enough. We could only finish in fourth place in my first season, the last Champions League position, which meant going into the qualifying rounds at the beginning of the following season. However, as I had only joined in November and had not had a full season and preseason, we did well to finish fourth. The next season Seedorf and Nesta arrived, along with others, such as Rivaldo. We already had Rui Costa, and these four players were key for me because I knew that, after Capello and his successors, the president wanted to change the style of the team a little bit. Capello's teams were really well organized, but maybe they didn't deliver the level or style that the president wanted. It would not be the last time I was to be tasked with changing a team's style to suit the owners and the fans.

With all of these new players joining, we had another difficulty, which was how to keep so many incredible players content. Not everyone could play every game, but that is exactly what talented players want to do. In midfield we would eventually have to accommodate Kaká, Gennaro Gattuso, Rui Costa, Andrea Pirlo, Seedorf and Rivaldo and up front we had Crespo, Andriy Shevchenko, Jon Dahl Tomasson and Filippo Inzaghi. The challenge was to keep them all happy while also thinking about developing the team. The atmosphere at Milan was good, which is incredibly important, and the players knew that they were in a fantastic team playing for a great club, so they became more willing to accept they wouldn't feature in every game. Of course, there were difficulties, but they were dealt with individually.

Early in my first full season we had a Champions League

game and Rivaldo, who hadn't had a full preseason or prep-aration for the match, was put on the bench. I tried to explain to him that he was going to play three days later, but he said, 'Rivaldo has never been on the bench.'

I told him, 'OK, there's always a first time, and now is the right time to be the first one.'

'No, no,' he said to me. 'Rivaldo doesn't go on the bench.'

I said, 'Rivaldo, you *have* to go on the bench.' He just got up and went home.

It is difficult for the truly special players to understand why they cannot play, even when they are only 80 per cent fit. They are great because they want to play every game, fit or injured. This is part of what makes a champion's person-ality. The club spoke to him, spoke with his agent, and he came back and went on the bench for the match against Modena, a small game. Only then did I speak with him again. I said, 'Listen, it's for you, not for us. You don't have to be worried because it can happen today, it can happen in the next game and it can happen to any player. We have a lot of games and it means you can be more fresh when you play in the next match.'

Up until this period, Milan had not been enjoying much success, but it was coming. We were building towards it. We won the Champions League in 2003 and success cemented the belief among the players that they were at a great club. They understood that sometimes they would play and sometimes they would not. It became easier to manage the big players because *all* the players were big.

Another challenge at a big club like Milan is managing the competition among players. In the beginning Christian Abbiati was the number one goalkeeper and Dida the number two. So, Dida had to wait. Luckily for him – and unluckily for his rival – Abbiati broke his rib and faced a spell out of the side. Dida stepped up in his absence, so that when Abbiati returned from injury I had to tell him that Dida had done well and would continue to play at number one. He took it well and stayed as number two for a while, until he was eventually moved on. This is the way at the big clubs. You have to wait for your chance and then take it. And, when you do take it, you have to know that you will always be challenged. There is no room for complacency at a big club and it is important for the players to know that, if they do well when they get the chance, they will get their opportunity in the team; Abbiati knew this well and was fully professional.

We had great times at Milan, winning two Champions Leagues and the Scudetto – the Serie A title – and I was at home with my football family, but eventually the relationship cooled and we both became a little tired. Eight years is a long time and Berlusconi wanted to change something. I did too. I wanted to try a new experience outside the country.

I had previously had a contract with Real Madrid all lined up, but I told the Spanish club, 'I leave Milan only if they want me to leave. I am ready to come to Madrid, but only if Milan allow me to go.' I even had a clause inserted that stated, 'This contract will become valid only once AC Milan gives its consent.' When I told Galliani about my opportunity he said, 'No, no, no – stay. You must stay.' So I did. Galliani had shown great faith in me, as had Madrid when they pursued me. Nothing is as important as being loved and valued.

The next year it was Chelsea and I had the same conversation with them: 'I'm going to speak with Milan and if Milan want me to stay, I stay.' When I spoke to Galliani this time, he was honest and said, 'It could be an idea.' It was time.

Exporting Success

Chelsea Boy

Chelsea initially courted me during two meetings in May 2008, in Geneva and Paris. The manager's position was soon to become vacant, as José Mourinho's replacement, Avram Grant, was due to be replaced himself. The need for the meetings to be clandestine affairs meant that this courtship took on a slightly comical turn, not least because the notion that any meetings between two people such as Roman Abramovich and me could be kept secret was immediately undermined within a couple of hours of the Paris meeting, when Adriano Galliani called me to ask how it had gone. I lost out on the job that time because the owner chose Luiz Felipe Scolari before me, supposedly because of my poor English.

Scolari proved to be not so effective for Chelsea and was sacked in early 2009. Guus Hiddink was hired as an emergency replacement until the end of the season and so suddenly I was back in the equation. The whole interview process was repeated, with further 'secret' meetings with Abramovich and his staff. In February 2009 Chelsea's director of football operations, Mike Forde, spent a series of meetings over a six-week period with me and my assistant, Bruno Demichelis. Unusually, for me, these discussions covered such issues as Chelsea's vision, the club's operating model, key strategic objectives, the use of data, performance modelling, managing the big players and the conditions I believed I needed to be successful at Chelsea. Mike questioned me in great depth about all these matters and more.

This courtship was very intense and unlike any I'd experienced with other clubs. In March I agreed to join, beginning my duties in June, and, after I signed, Mike gave me a great deal of help to understand the staff structure, the special features of the Premier League, Chelsea's recruitment policy and the expectations of the owner – though these had already been made very clear to me. I was taken to Holland, with Bruno, for an intense week-long course in English, solid days from eight in the morning until eight in the evening. If the language had been an issue the last time, I was determined that it would not be so this time; I like to be known as a good student so I studied hard. Soon after I started my duties, I held my first press conference at Chelsea and spoke English in front of over 200 journalists. I was nervous, of course, but very pleased.

The dressing room at Chelsea had many strong characters and I'm sure my own career success helped me at the beginning. When you join a club after winning two Champions Leagues, you tend to command a lot of respect from the players – but only at the beginning. This honeymoon period with the players never lasts long because immediately after that, they are looking at you and asking, 'What can this guy do for me?'

I didn't change the style of the training. The players felt comfortable with it as it was, so it seemed right to keep it. We did change the style of the play, though, and that helped in a different way because the players had to concentrate and learn, which always motivates the best of them. Of course, just as I would see later with Real Madrid, we had to change the way we played because the owner wanted something different about the style. On one of the first occasions I met Abramovich he told me, 'I want to find a manager that gives my team an identity, because when I watch Chelsea I'm not able to find an identity. When I see Barcelona or Manchester United, I find an identity in the team – when I watch Chelsea I cannot find an identity.' So we changed the style of play – we played with more possession. What better way to control possession than with a player like Milan's

Andrea Pirlo? We tried to sign him, but it was not possible, so in the beginning I played with Michael Essien in this position, who adapted and became one of the best in that position.

The beginning of my time at Chelsea was glorious. I took charge of the team for a preseason tour to the US and we won every game. My ideas, thoughts and approach seemed to be well received by the players. We started the season proper very well, with the team winning fourteen of the first sixteen games in all competitions. However, even then there were signs that the relationship with the owner might be difficult. During that great run of games, we lost 3–1 to Wigan. It was just a blip, to my mind, something that happens in football, but Abramovich came to the training ground the next morning to demand answers. I tried to listen and not respond impulsively, but maybe I should have had some answers ready for him and been more prepared. I should have recognized this as my first red flag. It was a new type of relationship for me with an owner – even Berlusconi had not been so demanding.

When December came around we were in the top two in the Premier League and had won our Champions League group. We then drew Inter Milan – and, of course, José Mourinho – in the last sixteen of the Champions League and the pressure and expectation began immediately, even though the games were over two months away. We started 2010 playing strongly in the FA Cup, but in February two thunderbolts hit me that would seriously affect my relationship with Abramovich. First, we were beaten 4–2 at home by Manchester City, which was bad because we were outfought and tactically outthought. He called a 9 a.m. meeting the next day to ask what had happened. Abramovich is never happy with these 'thunderbolt' defeats – defeats that he believes should not happen to Chelsea. The second, and worse, thunderbolt was our away defeat to Inter in the first leg of our Champions League tie.

When we lost to Inter again in the second leg, 1–0 at home, I was challenged publicly by the media for the first time. The honeymoon period was well and truly over. The next day Abramovich addressed the group, demanding answers. This was another episode which taught me how to deal with this different kind of president; again, I chose not to meet aggression with aggression, it is not my way. I like to think through difficult times, address the problems coolly and with reason. When Mourinho's Inter went on to win the competition – an ambition he was not able to fulfil when he was at Chelsea – it was not good for me. Perhaps this was the beginning of the end, a big red flag.

We were out of the Champions League but I challenged the players to achieve a new goal – to win the League and FA Cup double for the first time in Chelsea's history. I put up a chart that signposted our way to the achievement, telling them that in the twentieth century only four teams had won the double, and in the twenty-first century only one, and that we would be the first for eight years, since Arsenal in 2002. This became our new mission.

This is where building strong relationships comes into play. The players knew that the owner was on my case and they felt that they had let me down. They began playing for me; they felt that they owed me and they responded brilliantly.

We went on to win a lot of games, many of them by big margins – we scored a lot of goals – and, on the last day of the season, we beat Wigan 8–0 to win the League. A week later we won the FA Cup final against Portsmouth to complete the double. Unusually, I was not offered an extension to my three-year contract after the final. In fact, it was not even discussed. All of which suggested another red flag to me.

There were more worrying signs to come. There were no major new players brought in over the summer and several of the older players, such as Michael Ballack, were not offered new contracts. I was asked to promote five young academy graduate players into the twenty-five-man squad, which I did. We won the first game of the new season 6–0, but I was still summoned to Abramovich's house that night to receive a 'dressing down', as they say in England, for the performance. Another red flag – and only one game into the season.

We continued the strong start and we were top until we had a bad November. We lost to Liverpool, 2–0, and my assistant Ray Wilkins was fired days later. Another lesson learned. I could have fought harder, but I knew that it was a done deal. Michael Emenalo, the club's head of opposition scouting, was made assistant manager and I had to introduce him to the squad. The English players in particular were not happy with the way things had been done.

I was surprised when the club changed Wilkins. It was not discussed with me first. In my first year at the club Ray was, of course, important because of the language – he spoke Italian – and he was a good reference for the players. In my second year in the job, although I certainly didn't want to, I could do without him. The club had made the decision – Ray was already gone. When Abramovich decided to make Emenalo the assistant manager – *my* assistant – I told the club that I didn't need another assistant. I already had Paul Clement and Bruno Demichelis, and between us we had everything covered.

I didn't have any personal problem with Emenalo, but he was not comfortable in his new role. He was not used to being an assistant manager – his experience was in scouting – but the club put him there anyway. He was certainly not comfortable in front of the players, because they knew him from his time in a certain role, not in his new position.

In January the club made two marquee signings – Fernando Torres from Liverpool and David Luiz from Benfica – which lifted spirits, but not for long. Sadly, Torres was not at his best after a period of injury at Liverpool. In April we played Manchester United in the Champions League quarter-finals, with the feeling that we would have to win to save our season. The night before the second leg, Abramovich addressed the players, telling them they had to win or there would be huge changes to the team. He told me individually that if we lost then I was not to bother coming back to work. I wasn't sure if he was serious. We lost and I did go back to work, though I felt like a dead man walking. Again, I suppose I could have confronted the owner, but it seemed pointless.

We lost, 1–0 away at Everton, on the last day of the season. I'm told that the CEO was driving away from the stadium when he got the call to say, 'Turn around and tell Carlo he is fired.' I think the logic was that there was no point in waiting and telling me later. At least this way I could say goodbye to the players and staff before the off-season. That night, when the team arrived back in London, the senior players – Didier Drogba, John Terry, Frank Lampard and the others – took me out for dinner and a few drinks. I had never known that before in my career. I think I was liked.

My time at Chelsea followed a familiar arc. We delivered an amazing League and Cup double in the first season, playing in the style the owner wanted, followed by an inevitable hiatus, a cooling of the relationship with the owner and my possibly harsh dismissal. The time frame of the arc, after my long period at Milan, was new to me, however.

In the first season the results and the style seemed to please the owner, although, as I look back now, there were those red flags I mentioned that I had missed. In the second season I saw the end coming months before it did, just as I would later at Madrid. Rumours had begun to circulate that I gave more advantages to the English players than the others – that the English players were my favourites. This was not true. I had a fantastic relationship with the English players because they were very professional and 'energizers' in the squad. I didn't care what happened outside of that because in the period when things were getting serious, they were really good on the pitch.

The relationship with the owner, however, was not so good. To break a relationship there are little details that all add up. There was the sacking and replacing of Ray Wilkins, and Abramovich also started to say that I had a preference for certain players; perhaps he was buying into the rumours about my favouritism. I told him that it wasn't true – I made it very clear. It is important that presidents and coaches can be open with each other.

Maybe the favouritism thing was an excuse for Abramovich. I believe his main reason for letting me go was that he thought the management of the squad was not right. He thought that I was too kind in front of the players and he grew sure that it was causing something to go wrong within the group. He would try to convince me, with all my experience to the contrary, to be stronger, tougher and more rigorous with the players.

I'd heard it before and I've heard it since, but he was wrong – they are all wrong. I don't change my character.

What they hire me for is my ability to calm the situation at a club by building relationships with the players, which is one of my biggest strengths. At some later stage that is not the approach they want any more and the relationship with the owners – not the players, but the owners – begins to worsen. They hire me to be kind and calm with the players and then at the first sign of trouble along the way that's the very characteristic they point to as the problem. I know that if I am winning then it is because I am calm; equally, if I am losing it is because I am calm. How can it be both? It's a paradox, but I was trapped by it at Chelsea. Maybe this is the natural cycle of managers in general, that the very reason they are hired in the first place eventually becomes the reason they are fired. Or maybe this is only the reason for the Ancelotti arc. I know that I cannot change my character, so maybe I cannot change my arc. All I can say for certain is that I was very disappointed to leave Stamford Bridge.

The Parisian Project

Paris Saint-Germain had been acquired by Qatar Sports Investments under the chairmanship of Nasser Al-Khelaifi, and they were looking for a big-name coach to lead the team to new heights, especially in the Champions League. As a Champions League winner, my name will always be on the list in such a situation, but to offer me the position was widely considered strange in France as Paris Saint-Germain were sitting at the top of Ligue 1 at the time.

Paris Saint-Germain didn't question me, as Mike Forde

had done at Chelsea, about my style of coaching, philosophies or staffing needs. Perhaps this was because the general director there was my friend from Milan, Leonardo. Paris Saint-Germain was to be a new challenge for me. Their vision was to become one of the best sides in Europe in two or three years and it was my job to manage the project and deliver that goal.

I joined the club in December 2011, midway through the season. When you become manager during the season it's difficult to bond with the existing staff, because there hasn't been time before the competitions start to develop a way of working together. To have a full preseason with the staff and players is so important for building relationships. Timing is crucial. What is the situation? What are the constraints? Is it best to avoid joining a business mid-season, in a mid-budget cycle? Was I asking for trouble?

I realized very quickly that PSG didn't have good organization, so I had to bring in staff. It was back to my previous working pattern. I brought in Paul Clement as my assistant along with a new physical trainer, analysts and scientists. At Chelsea I already had capable experts to cover the most important areas, but for me PSG was a new challenge where I had to build my own support team.

It wasn't just the staff that needed organizing. The club was so different from Milan or Chelsea, where everything is in place and they know how to manage things. PSG was more like the clubs I'd managed early in my career, rather than one with ambitions to be a global superclub. We travelled to an away fixture and, on the Thursday, the team administrator asked us what we wanted to eat on Saturday night: 'Do you want salmon or chicken?' What? You are asking me this on a Thursday – why isn't it already established? The club didn't even have a restaurant. The players would arrive at the ground thirty minutes before training and leave immediately afterwards.

I needed to introduce the conditions and organization that would help build the kind of winning mentality that the big clubs all possess. The players needed to understand, as those at Milan had done, that they were part of a great club – but I had to begin this process slowly, slowly, softly, softly. I spoke with the players about what we would do and, day by day, we began to improve the culture of the club. We organized a small restaurant in the training ground for the players to have breakfast when they arrived and lunch after training, so that they could be together and develop some team spirit. We didn't impose any of this. We just organized things for the players and made it welcoming for them to stay, so that they would *want* to stay.

Despite having been top of the league when I was approached, we finished second, a situation in which the coach would usually be sacked. I wasn't, and I felt very encouraged by this. The club's board were focused on the project and they seemed to understand that it would take time. You have to buy players in the summer, build a squad and then win the league next year, reach maybe the quarter-final of the Champions League. It was essential for me both to improve the team the year after and to improve it year on year, and it was a positive sign that I was being given the time to do this.

We began to bring in players with the right mentality. In the summer we signed Zlatan Ibrahimović and Thiago Silva, both top players and highly professional. They were examples for the others. Sometimes it's the players who have to be the leaders, not the manager, and Silva and Ibrahimović immediately became the leaders in the dressing room. It was why I wanted them.

I spoke with Ibrahimović separately and explained the situation at the club and how important he could be in the dressing room. 'You can be a good example for all the others,' I said. 'You have experience, talent, personality; you have character and in this sense you can be fantastic.'

Maybe he's not so diplomatic, but he's a winner. The biggest problem I had with him was on the training ground. Even at the training sessions he didn't want to lose anything – ever. He's always fighting, always 100 per cent. He can only be one way – direct. If he doesn't like something, he's going to tell you. With the young players he could be too strong, so I told him that he had to take care of them because he was an example for them. I explained that a bit of subtlety was required, as it is not always effective to speak so strongly with the young. Subtlety is not Ibra's strongest suit.

One day on the training ground, Ibra thought that one of the young players had not given his best effort to the session. At the end of training Ibra called this guy over and said, 'Now, you have to go home and write in your diary that you trained with Zlatan today, because I think it could be the last time that you do.'

He was never afraid to speak the truth to anyone, even me. On one occasion we were speaking about Hernán Crespo, who was, in my opinion, an outstanding striker. When I asked Ibra what he thought, he said, 'Yes, he's a striker, but he cannot make the difference. There are only three players who make the difference: Ibrahimović, Messi and Ronaldo.' Such is his confidence and he is correct to think it. Ibra is one of the few strikers, maybe the only one, who is just as happy when he makes an assist as he is when he scores. He is one of the most unselfish players I have ever met, which is of massive value to the team.

With all of the new arrivals over the summer, it took time for them to settle in and become embedded in their role, so even by the December of my first full season, the team was still not in the right shape. Despite this, we were well placed in second position in the league and we had qualified for the knockout stages of the Champions League with a game to spare. Then we lost a game against Nice. We were due to play the last group game in the Champions League three days later when the president and Leonardo came to tell me, 'If you don't win this game you will be sacked.' We had already qualified from the group, so why would he say this then, even if it was true?

They came again, the day before the match, and both told

me, 'Win tomorrow or the sack.' When I asked why, they said, 'Because we are not happy. We are following the project, not only the result, and we're not happy. We've decided that if we don't win this game you will be sacked.'

I told them that even if they thought that, why tell a manager he will be sacked? If I win the game what happens then? I stay, sure, but I won't be comfortable. I will know that I've lost the confidence of the president and the general director.

We won the game. We played well, beating Porto 2–1, so I wasn't sacked. But everything had changed for me. I no longer had the trust of the club, which made my position untenable, especially in a long-term project like this one, and I told Leonardo that, at the end of the season, I would go. Leonardo was my friend, or so I had thought, and he gave no real explanation for treating me like that. I was surprised, because it should never happen like this in football, or in any business. If you have to sack people then sack them – don't tell them that if they lose or do a bad job you're *going* to sack them. If I don't do a good job then just fire me, but don't give me stupid ultimatums. You are the boss, so of course you have the right to sack whoever you want – just be a man about it.

It was the opposite at Juventus, where I signed a new contract but when we finished the season in second place, the club was not happy. They called me and said, 'We have to change the manager.' Up until the last day I was thought to be the best manager in the world for them, and the next day they let me go. OK, no problem – but don't tell me this *during* the season.

I'm not sure that the prevailing orthodoxy in HR would agree with me, but I want to be honest. I'd always prefer losing my job not to be dragged out. I've learned that getting sacked – and getting recruited, for that matter – is rarely just about you. It is always about the person hiring or firing you. Do your job to the best of your ability and let others judge you because they will anyway.

I was sad to leave PSG because of the relationship I had established with the players, but it had become impossible for me to stay. Another arc had drawn to a close, which was disappointing and surprising, because I had expected to be involved in a long-term project. However, an exciting new challenge was awaiting me in Madrid.

Great Expectations: Real Madrid

It was an acceptable start. In my first season at Real Madrid I delivered the holy grail of 'La Décima' – a record tenth European Cup/UEFA Champions League title – for the club's president, Florentino Pérez. I managed to integrate record-signing Gareth Bale into a role that added value to the team and complemented Cristiano Ronaldo; I oversaw Ángel Di María's rediscovery of his form and I resurrected Luka Modrić, who had become possibly the most important player after Ronaldo.

As the second season began, things just seemed to get

better. We went on an unprecedented twenty-two-match winning run, only to succumb to injuries and politics and eventually win nothing. So, just twelve months after delivering the Champions League at the first attempt, I paid the price – with my job.

As Vito Corleone would have said in one of my favourite movies, *The Godfather*: 'It's not personal, it's just business.'

Two years before, I was sad to be leaving Paris Saint-Germain after winning Ligue 1 in France. But I knew that I was on my way to one of the most coveted and precarious leadership challenges in world football at Madrid. Florentino Pérez had never hidden his admiration for me, having made an approach twice before to make me Real manager, and when I finally joined at the third time of asking, he welcomed me and what he called the calming presence of the 'peacemaker'.

He said many kind words, but I also knew that the same Pérez had presided over the hirings and firings of nine managers in his twelve years over two terms as president. My eyes were wide open from the start – it's the nature of the job – and, as was clear from Pérez's statements immediately after sacking me, Madrid is not a club where you should be putting down roots. Even by football's crazy standards, Madrid are in a class of their own. The time to adjust, the honeymoon and the time to sustain success is even more compressed than in the rest of football. When he sacked me Pérez said, 'Carlo is part of our history because he won "La Décima" for us. But here the demands are very high and we need to give Real Madrid a new push that allows us to reach the level that we want to be. It was a very difficult decision to make. The demands at this club are the utmost because Madrid always wants to win silverware.'

His words were kind at the end too, when he added that the 'affection that the players and the fans have for Carlo is the same as the affection I myself have for him'. Only two days before Pérez's announcement Cristiano Ronaldo had tweeted, 'Great coach and amazing close relationships that Ancelotti has built with the players. I hope we work together next season.' Other players had followed suit, so I could be pleased that I had made positive relationships, which is always an important goal for me. Relationships with my staff, my players, the general manager and, of course, the president – they're vital.

The most important thing when I started the job in Madrid was to calm the dressing room following Mourinho's departure. Many of the players were unsettled and I needed to build relationships with the senior players quickly. It is important for me to identify the leaders in the team, and the different types of leader, so I can work well with them. Players like Sergio Ramos, Ronaldo, Pepe – they were already the leaders.

Ronaldo is what I call a 'technical leader', who leads by example; he doesn't speak a lot but is serious, very professional and takes care of himself. He is a good guy. Ramos is what I call a 'personality leader', a leader with strong character, who is never scared, never worried – always positive. Pepe is a fantastic and serious player. His energy and drive are infectious. Iker Casillas was also important as he was always, man and boy, a Madridista. He and the fans he represented believed that he had been badly treated, so it was important to have him onside. These were the people I wanted the other players to look to, to reference. For example, I remember a small incident with Fábio Coentrão, when he complained that another player was not working hard enough. I asked him, 'Who do you compare yourself to? Is it to the player who is not working or the sixteen who are?' Straight away, he knew. Reference the leaders because they are the ones who will help your career.

Madrid is an amazing organization with great history and tradition. At Paris Saint-Germain I was maybe the most important part of the project because I had the experience that nobody else had, but at Real Madrid you are only ever a piece of the project, because everyone in the organization knows what they are there to do. Everyone from the kit man to the president is able to work at the top level. Real Madrid is like AC Milan, the club I've called home before, apart from with the manager, which Madrid change a lot. All the other people – the kit man, the physio – they are more or less the same over a long period of time, like a family, working together. So, the support staff are permanent, which was good for me. I didn't have to concern myself with that, it was already in place, so I was able to say to the players, 'Let's just concentrate on getting better.'

At Real Madrid it is not possible to complete a season without winning the one trophy or even the many trophies that the president has promised the fans and the media. In my first season he had promised 'La Décima', which we delivered and also we won the Copa del Rey, but I knew that the president only really cared about the Champions League. It had become an obsession with everybody around the club. They had hired the 'special one' to secure 'La Décima', yet even someone so special had failed to deliver it.

They had been playing a more defensive style than the president liked before I arrived, so, while I was given the freedom to change the style of play, it was insisted of me, whether I wanted to or not, that we should be more offensive. Thankfully, I was experienced in working with a president's wishes and any leader needs to become comfortable with the particular demands of their position. It worked well for me. The team was more motivated because when you change the style of play the players listen and concentrate more and work harder in training. For the same reason I changed a lot of the training sessions and kept switching them regularly. I didn't want to do the same exercises all the time because it becomes monotonous quickly. It all went well initially, but gradually we had to start to make decisions about where to put our efforts. Should we rest players? Should we concentrate on the Champions League or La Liga? We managed it effectively, winning the Champions League and making the obsession of the club a reality. But already, the pressure for the next season begins. A club like Madrid never stands still.

We want to win the Champions League again, of course, but we can't let Barcelona and Atlético Madrid finish ahead of us again in La Liga. I'm often asked if I consider the second season a failure because we didn't win any trophies and I got sacked. I say, 'No. Things were going well, we'd won twenty-two consecutive games, and then we had two big issues.'

The first was a problem caused by statistics, which 'revealed' that our players were not working hard enough compared with other top European sides. The medical data turned out to be based on analysis by UEFA, which showed Real Madrid used less training time to prepare for games than other top European teams. The implication was that we should increase our workload in training.

The numbers were wrong. We'd won twenty-two games in a row so we must have been doing something right. But we'd just broken that winning streak when the stats were released, and sometimes to explain a defeat people have to make something specific responsible for it, instead of thinking more coolly about it. (My preference is to find a solution, not to look for the guilty to blame.) The club jumped on that as an explanation and demanded more work.

The club wanted to put pressure on the players, saying, 'We need to work – we have to work harder, we have to have more concentration before the games.' But it was wrong – I actually needed to give the players more rest. We suffered for about a month with injuries and fatigue, which was crucial to losing La Liga. We lost against Barcelona during this period and I had five important players injured – Sergio Ramos, James Rodríguez, Pepe, Luka Modrić and Karim Benzema – between February and March. We suffered especially from the injuries to Modrić and Benzema, because we didn't have clear replacements for their very specific roles and talents. Even though we won nine out of our last ten games, it was too late. We had already lost the league.

The issue with the medical data was a big signal that the club's faith in my ability to do the job had lessened. It showed that they had more trust in the numbers than in me, and it was around this time that the second issue arose. One morning in March I received a phone call from the general director, saying that the president wanted to speak with me at the end of training that day. This was very unusual. When I visited the president, he told me that Gareth Bale's agent had been to his office to speak about the 'Bale situation'. Earlier in the year, on 4 January, I'd substituted Bale in the match that brought our winning streak to an end, and the president was reported as saying, 'To remove Bale is to attack me,' and, 'Once he [Ancelotti] removed him [Bale] and I reproached him but Carlo didn't understand it. Since then he lost my confidence.'

In January Bale's agent had been saying things and perhaps felt his position was strong because he had already spoken with the president. Now he was telling the president that Bale was unhappy in his position. He wanted to play more centrally. The president asked me what we were going to do and I told him, 'Nothing.' It was impossible to change his position at that stage of the season because I would have had to change the whole system and move many more players around. I also told the president that I was surprised the player could not speak directly with me. That would be normal. I would have expected the player to come to see me because I don't want to speak with agents. I try to avoid speaking with agents at all. Later in the season, in response to more comments from Bale's agent, I said in the press that sometimes it's good for agents to be quiet, to shut up.

Bale had fantastic world class qualities and all that I was trying to do was help him understand his core strengths so he could fulfil his potential and by the way, that I was more qualified than his agent or the president to help him with that. I like to work with players to do the best for them and the team. Once before, for example, I had the problem of fitting four great players, Pirlo, Seedorf, Rui Costa and Kaká into three places for my team. I spent time talking to all of them and I told them they had to work it out or one of them every game would be on the bench. Eventually *we* came up with the diamond where Pirlo and Kaká exchanged places, Pirlo deeper and Kaká more forward. That 4-4-2 system turned Kaká into the World Player of the Year by him playing at the top of a diamond and, simultaneously, scoring more and creating more assists while allowing the team to win.

I told the president that I would speak with Bale myself the next day, which I did after training. I told him, 'I know that your agent spoke to the president. Why didn't you come to speak with me about what you want?' He said, 'Yes, OK, no problem.' I explained to him what I had said to the president, how it was impossible for me to change the system as it wasn't just one position, it was the whole team. I was clear with him. I told him that we could try some things in the summer, next year's preseason, to change his position, but not now. It didn't make sense; we had found a shape that worked and in which he'd had a great first season. In my opinion, it was not the moment to change the shape. To be able to have the wide players swap sides, to switch the play, was central to our style of football. Whenever you play with two wingers, such as we were with Ronaldo and Bale, to be able to change sides as quickly as they can is the most important thing.

Sometimes players who arrive at the top level because of particular skills believe that they want to do things differently, they want to experiment to try to be better. They forget what enabled them to reach the top level in the first place. I had one player, for example, who was powerful, physical – he could sprint a hundred times without tiring – he was all about power and pace, which was what helped him win the Ballon d'Or. But then he started to think that he was a different kind of talent than he was and he stopped working so hard, stopped running so hard – all the things that had made him great – and this affected his career. He is still a big friend of mine so I can say this and he would admit that it was true. A manager has to work with the player to try to get him to be clear about his development; to understand what makes him great.

Anyway, from that moment on the relationship with the president was not the same. At the end of the season things were actually feeling positive, even though we had won nothing. We had reached the semi-final of the Champions League, we had broken records and my relationship with the players was a happy one. The new players were bedded in and the other important members of the team would soon be returning from injury. I was very confident that we were in an excellent position to challenge for all competitions the next season, with only a few small adjustments necessary, but I guess the president's mind had already been made up. At Madrid, the signals of the ending were the same as at Chelsea; they start not to discuss the future, not to make plans; it is a different feeling, the relationship feels different.

As we now know, there was to be no 'next season' for me at Madrid. When the news came that my reign at the Berna-béu was at an end, I had, despite my confidence for the future, been expecting it for some weeks. It wasn't the first time I'd been fired and it probably won't be the last. Being sacked or leaving a club is part of this job and as a manager you know from the beginning that it is a reality.

The most difficult aspect about it ending at Madrid – as at any club – was leaving behind the relationships I had forged with my players. However, I always remain on good terms with them and our relationships tend to last.

My time at Real was shorter than I'd hoped, but also longer than many who manage there. It is difficult to say if things might have been different. They wanted the players to train harder. However, as I did not agree I continued to conduct my training sessions exactly as I had planned, without changing my ideas. Leading may sometimes involve compromise, especially at the biggest clubs, but not when it comes to your expertise and you have the conviction of your decisions. While this might have helped us win another trophy, or bought more time, it does feel that this arc, the rise and fall, is somehow inevitable throughout my career.

LEADERSHIP ARC: THE QUIET WAY

- The leadership arc may be personal, not generic. Your various job arcs may be more about you than the jobs. This should be a serious consideration when deciding whether or not to accept a job.

- The transition from member of staff to leader is not as straightforward as you think. You have to understand that, no matter how insignificant you think your actions and words are, to your staff you cast a shadow over most aspects of their lives. Take that responsibility seriously; take care of people and don't abuse your power.

- The constraints on running an organization are not always on public view. Again, when deciding on a new role you must do as much due diligence as possible. It is no good complaining that you were 'sold a pup' if you haven't done your homework.

- Sometimes a relationship just gets tired and it's time to move on. Don't over internalize this, everything has a cycle. The key is to be as productive as possible in each cycle.

- Speaking truth to power has to be an acceptable behaviour. Leaders have to enable it for their own benefit. It is not a 'nice to have', it is essential.
- Find a solution, don't waste time looking for the guilty.
- You get a very short honeymoon period when you start a new job – make it count.
- Respect is everything. It is a daily currency that can go up and down in direct relation to your behaviour and choices. Take it seriously.
- Don't always be obsessed with drawing loyalty from the people with whom you work. Aim to inspire greater performance in the moment and focus on showing that you really care about them as people and their professional growth.
- Mutual trust comes as the final piece of the relationship pyramid but demonstrate *you* can be trusted from day one of your relationship with their talent.

IN THEIR OWN WORDS . . . THE PLAYERS

CRISTIANO RONALDO ON CARLO

I had always thought Carlo had such a tough-looking face – he looks like a tough guy in all of the photos I had seen of him – so, when I met him for the first time, it was a huge surprise because I didn't expect him to be such a good guy. He told me about his plans – what he wanted, what he thought about me – and he made me feel very comfortable. Over the next few days he began to show his personality, the way he works, the way he is as a person – not just with the players but with the staff and his employers at the club – and then you begin to understand why everyone speaks so highly about him.

In my opinion part of this is because of the way he is with people – he's very humble, which is not so normal in the football business. He treats everybody as an equal. He never dismisses someone just because they are not at his level; he will always listen.

Everyone has weaknesses. Because he is such a humble person it is very difficult to speak like this about him and the only weakness I can think of is also one of his great strengths. He is so very nice all the time and he never gets upset for more than a minute. He can tell you strongly about something he is not happy with, then it is done. This can be a weakness because if you are too nice, people might start to think they can take advantage of you. But it's a positive weakness, if you know what I mean, and I certainly don't look on him as being weak.

It shows that what he feels inside, in his heart, is always positive. This is good because it is honest. Working with honest people – not just in my job, but in any job – is very important. It's difficult to find honest, serious and sensitive people. Carlo likes to show a hard face to the world but inside he is an unbelievable person. He's one of the best and most important people that I have met in my entire time in football. With Carlo it's like a family – you become a part of his family.

I like to think that Carlo and I share some qualities; I see some of him in me. I believe that I am a sensitive person too. I sometimes show a tough or even arrogant face to the world, but I'm not like that with the people I love and those who work with me. Carlo helped me a lot and I wish he had stayed longer at Real Madrid. I hope to work with him again one day. Someone said to me, 'Will you be learning German?' I say, 'Toni Kroos has taught me a few words, but if one day I have to learn more German then I will learn.'

I have only seen Carlo angry a few times. When he loses his temper he shouts and screams in whatever language comes first to his mind and then, one minute after, he stops, catches his breath and goes outside. Then he returns, smoking a cigarette and totally calm – everything's fine again.

His ability to regain calmness very quickly is important. He knows how to talk to people and to deal with the bad moments. Even if you had lost a match the day before, he would say, 'Come on, guys, everything's going to be OK. We haven't lost anything yet – we just lost a game.' He was like that with us and with the staff too, which made the environment here at Madrid spectacular. For me, the atmosphere with Carlo was one of his most brilliant achievements. If you look at the two years under him and what we won – the Champions League, the Copa del Rey – it shows how important Carlo was for Real Madrid and for the players. When he left the club, many of us took to social media to say how much he meant to us all. He is an unbelievable person.

One of the reasons the atmosphere was so good was because he protected the dressing room from the president and anything else that might upset the balance of the family. I've seen that with my own eyes. People can say whatever they want, but I've seen that he doesn't bow down to pressure from anyone; he makes his own decisions – sometimes good, sometimes bad – which is always the way in the coach's job. This is why I like him, because he is his own man, with his own personality, his own choices, and he makes his decisions and sticks by them.

He's also smart – very smart in how he listens to the players. He understands players – he was one once, so he has the experience. He knows how to get the most out of the team to win games and trophies. It's not a coincidence that we won almost everything. He has the plan and the strategy. If you don't do the right things, you're not going to win anything. As much as he would listen to the players, he would always make what he believed was the right decision. If the difference was to move one player to a different position or move another, he would look at the consequences and then move the player that caused the least disruption to the team. He would not move five players if he could achieve the same results by moving just one.

Although he treats all the players the same, he also understands that, as in any sport or job, he needs to treat the special players not differently, but with more care. At the end of the day, it's good for the team that you use the players as effectively as you can. Even when you maybe feel that you haven't got the strength to last the whole ninety minutes, or you feel that you can't run any more, then you need to do it for the coach. I will do it for him, because he deserves it as he has always taken care of me. Most of my teammates feel the same – players admire him and will hurt for him.

You can see this in the way I played in the Champions League final in 2014. I was injured a month before the game and he said to me a few times, 'Cristiano, if you don't feel good, just let me know. It will be tough on me because even if you are only fifty per cent you're still our most important player.' So I played. I didn't play unbelievably well, but I scored a penalty – my seventeenth goal in the Champions League that season, a record – and we won the competition. I wasn't fully fit, but I made the sacrifice for Carlo.

Every player should be humble and know that they don't know everything about football. I always look to learn and take some pointers from every coach. I take a point off this one, a point off that one, because they know – they are older and have the experience. They are not going to teach me how to play football or how to kick the ball, but if you are smart, you can take advantage of every coach and learn about many things that, in my opinion, are important. With Carlo, he develops even the best players by continually making them motivated to work for him. He always motivates me. He would say, 'Bomba' – he calls me Bomba, which is Italian for bomber – 'Let's go – today you're

going to score a goal; you are going to win us the game, Bomba.'
Even when I didn't score a goal in the first half, he would speak
to me in the dressing room at half-time. 'You're going to score,'
he'd say. 'You're playing unbelievable.' He was always giving me
confidence, all the time, and for me the most important thing is
that he cares for me. He would always take care of me. These
qualities are why every club wants him. He's a special coach.

Journalists often ask me about my coaches. Some of them
have many similarities, of course. Carlo and Sir Alex Ferguson,
for example – they are very similar. They both create a family;
they are different kinds of parents but with the same thoughts
about protecting you and enabling you to express your talent.
Tactics weren't the main thing with either of them. Even with
Carlo there was not that much emphasis on tactics, even though
he had worked in Italy. Before he arrived at Madrid, we were all
thinking that as an Italian he would have a strong emphasis on a
lot of tactical training sessions, but the training started with
Carlo – and no tactics. He said, 'With this team, I don't need a lot
of tactics. I want to score goals with these players.' When you
have this mentality, to attack, the emphasis shifts away from
defensive training. Of course, you must still have quality organization, but not tactics in the way that tactics are usually used,
such as when making a counter-attacking team. Carlo is not like

that. Other players have told me that he worked hard on tactics at other clubs, but not here at Real Madrid, no.

Maybe this was because at AC Milan or Paris Saint-Germain he didn't have the players that he had at Real Madrid – skilful players, driven players. I think that the most important thing is concentration. When you concede goals at set pieces this is about concentration, not tactics. If a guy is faster than you and jumps higher than you, this is not tactics. So, it's about concentration, and Carlo was very aware of this. Obviously, he is an organized person and he is very flexible. If he didn't have the quality of player that we have at Real Madrid, maybe he would have spent more time on tactics.

Where Carlo and Ferguson were very family oriented, José Mourinho was a little bit different, more distant. Carlo was closer to us and took more care of the players. What all three of these managers have in common, though, is their huge knowledge of the game. The three of them are very smart and they are all winners, it's as simple as that. Even with all that knowledge, the key for them is the relationships they build. Each is aware that only by having great relationships can you get the best from the players. That is what is special about them. I have played for and with the best so I have been blessed.

You can tell how good a guy is when he is on the training pitch.

In my opinion, Carlo is one of the best out there. He has a sixth sense about when players are tired or bored, or want to work more or less hard. When Zizou [Zinedine Zidane] arrived with us after Benítez, the training was very similar to that with Carlo. Zizou understood that for him, as a player, Carlo's sessions had been enjoyable and valuable, so he employed similar methods. Zizou is a smart guy and he took a lot of ideas from his time with Carlo both as a player and as his assistant here at Madrid. The most important thing is that Zizou has tried to keep the same mood as Carlo.

Carlo would joke a lot, sometimes about being angry or to make you worry. He would sometimes say to me, 'Cristiano, tomorrow you're going to rest.' Everyone knows I want to play every game, so I would be upset and say, 'What are you talking about?' He would tell me I must rest and we would go back and forth and then he would say, 'You must rest at three o'clock tomorrow . . . but when the game starts at four, you can play.' And then he would laugh.

Carlo knows when it's time to have fun and when it's time to work and be serious. He always finds the right balance because of his knowledge, his experience. He's an intelligent coach because he cares and wants the best for you.

PART TWO
The Core Business

CHRIS BRADY

Fortune magazine's cover story for 21 June 1999 read 'Why CEOs Fail'. The simple answer was: by not getting things done. The article argued that leaders of major businesses were overly focused on 'strategy, missions and visions' and were paying insufficient attention to results (also ignoring their colleagues who were critical in delivering those results). As Herb Kelleher of Southwest Airlines succinctly put it, 'Strategy, overdone; doing stuff, underdone; our strategy, do stuff.'

When Lou Gerstner arrived at IBM, charged with sorting out the mess left by the outgoing CEO, he famously stated: 'The last thing IBM needs right now is a vision.' Gerstner removed few of the existing senior team but, significantly, he did replace the HR director. Gerstner understood that successful CEOs are invariably those who are interested in people. As the *Fortune* article concludes, 'The motto of successful CEOs: People first, strategy second.'

I spent ten years researching employee engagement; the results were published in 2007 in *The Extra Mile*, a book I co-wrote with David MacLeod. We found that concentration on getting things done, and managers who can deliver the 'people first' mantra, are crucial to the success of any business. So, as we have investigated the core business of football – what actually happens on the pitch – it is refreshing to know that Carlo Ancelotti and his quiet leadership are the embodiment of those beliefs. He is unwaveringly interested in and committed to the people under his leadership.

The new skills-based football economy chews up the talented, both players and managers, like no other; understanding that and managing it with dignity is also an Ancelotti trait. When speculation about his job at Madrid was rife, he was asked at a press conference about his future. He replied:

> I'd like to stay, but I don't know if I will be here next season . . .
> it's not up to me to give myself a grade for this year, it's up to
> others. I know very well how things are in football. I don't have
> to talk. If the club is happy, I can continue; if not, they will have to
> take a decision. The club has the right to change coach if it is not
> happy.

This statement was not bravado or obfuscation; it was genuine. Ancelotti understands, probably better than anybody working in the most cut-throat businesses, the transient nature of employment in any talent-dependent industry.

Those who are loath to regard football as an industry should pay attention to the words of Real Madrid general director José Ángel Sánchez, who says: 'We are a content producer.' In other words, Madrid and the other behemoths of modern sport have become commercial enterprises with sports clubs attached. This concept is validated by other distinguished names in both business and sport. Thomas J. Watson, the founder of IBM, once said, 'Business is a game, the greatest game in the world if you know how to play it,' while Clive Woodward, English rugby's only World Cup winning coach, put it like this: 'There's a complete parallel with running a successful company as there is running a successful sports team; you need the same skills.' Football really is the quintessential model for modern talent-dependent industries.

In this section Carlo reflects on all aspects of the core business, from culture to responsibilities, from dealing with the hierarchy to the shape of the working environment, from handling the talent to creating the product and, finally, to understanding the analytics and psychology that will comprise the next generation of competitive advantages.

2. Culture

The Family

Nothing is as important as family. In football there are two forms of family. There is my personal set of trusted lieutenants and staff, people I have worked with over the years, sharing the good times and the bad – people I have great trust in and respect for. They are my football family, and I will talk about these people shortly. Then there is the club as a family.

When I joined Milan as manager, it was like coming home for me. The club is set up exactly like a family, despite being one of the grandest football teams in the world. You have your own room at Milanello, the training ground, and the kit man, the other staff – they have been there a very long time. There is a restaurant at Milanello and it's not a buffet, as it is at Chelsea and Real Madrid, but a proper restaurant with a waiter who comes to speak with you as a friend. The waiters at Milanello are mostly very old – they too have been there a long time – and the atmosphere is very easy. When I started to work on the organization and setup at Paris Saint-Germain, introducing a restaurant was one of my first priorities. I knew from my time in Milan how important it was for the players to have meals together, to help form a tighter unit. I wanted to bring the family environment I knew so well from Milan to Paris, and meal-times are an important part of family life. This is how I like the culture of the club to be and I consider the family atmosphere fundamental to success.

From the manager to the kit man, everyone needs to be part of this family and to work towards the shared object-ives. The key to the success of any organization is to align the whole family in the same direction. The players are an integral part of this and it is not helpful if there are dissent-ers who are working against the spirit of the family or who do not consider themselves to be part of it. It is my job to make sure that the family values, whatever they might be, are honoured and respected.

It was easy for me, coming back to Milan, having been a successful player for them and the club being so familiar to me, and sometimes I think that it might have been a prob-lem for Milan in that they were maybe too grateful to someone who played such a part in the history of the club.

So this is the culture of the club – a family setup. At other clubs it can be different. At Juventus it was like a company for me. When a club is like a company my relationship with my superiors is more formal. During my time at Juve we did not have our own training ground and facilities; we did not have our own 'home'. However, my experience at Juventus was still a good one in my mind. The results were not great during my time at the club, but you cannot always control the results. This does not mean that my relationship with the team was bad. The things over which I had control were working. Maybe the fans might not agree, but I cannot control them either.

It's important that the manager is a cultural fit for the club, as his job is to be an example for this culture, to maintain its standards and see that it is observed throughout the organization. For Milan, I was, of course, a natural fit, but at Juventus I was not. The family environment is better suited to who I am, and it is always easier to work in an atmosphere akin to who you are. Business guru Peter Drucker said, 'Culture eats strategy for breakfast,' and I agree. Without an empathy with the culture success can still be achieved, but it can also be fleeting, hard to sustain.

Wherever I go, I am always myself. My personality or style does not change, and ultimately I am hired for who I am. The prevailing atmosphere in the club when I arrive dictates the amount of time and work it will take me to achieve the atmosphere I desire, to create my family. This is why sometimes the most important job is to build this family atmosphere if it doesn't exist naturally. At a club like Chelsea, for example, it was also more like a company, but I saw it as an opportunity to build a family there.

When hiring leaders it is essential that the people hiring them know exactly the role they want the new leader to play – is it to maintain the culture or to create a new one? Interestingly, it is said that Sir Alex Ferguson was hired to revive a culture that had waned at Manchester United.

Having done so, he maintained his success by constantly reinforcing that culture, continually referencing the history and tradition of the club.

Of course, a manager can change their approach to fit the demands of the club, but it is easier to fit the coach to the club than the other way around – unless, of course, you want a change or there is a big reason to abandon your beliefs. If, for example, a big club wanted to break the monopoly of their biggest rival and they thought they could only achieve that with a manager who had already been successful at another club, but who maybe didn't fit culturally, they will in some cases overlook the fact that he won't adapt culturally, because the success is the top priority. When the club employed me they knew that I could adapt, but also I was, perhaps, closer to the Madrid that Florentino Pérez wished to resurrect. For him, the *galácticos* concept was crucial, and he believed my skill in forging relationships with the players was central to handling the different needs of the high-profile and strong personalities in that dressing room.

He was correct to believe this. However, the problem is that clubs rarely do enough interviewing and due diligence to be able to know everything about the incoming candidate. I believe Pérez made the correct decision when hiring me, but it is not always the way in football. In my career there was only one club – apart from Milan, who already knew me – where I was asked, 'How do you manage? How do you work with the players? What is your style of training? How would you deal with this situation and that situation?' This was Chelsea. I had ten meetings with Chelsea, which is the correct way to do business for me, but it is certainly not normal in football. All clubs should take note of this approach.

The likes of Pep Guardiola and Hungarian coach Béla Guttmann have said that three years is the natural cycle for managers, and my experience with my leadership arcs, one club aside, certainly backs this up. However, sometimes managers, players, coaches and workers find a natural home. Valeriy Lobanovskyi at Dynamo Kiev, Sir Alex Ferguson at Manchester United, Arsène Wenger at Arsenal, me at Milan – in these cases the relationship can last much longer than the three years. The manager has found a home and the club has found the right cultural fit. People say that this type of longevity will never happen again and it's easy to see why in today's game, but if a manager can find a home that is right for him and the club feel the same way, then who knows where it could lead?

International Culture

I have managed great teams all over Europe, highly diverse, multinational groups of players and backroom staff. Working in such an environment presents a unique set of linguistic challenges. Of course, you could say football is a language we all have in common – but it is vital that we are literally speaking the same language too.

I was a foreigner in England, as well as in Spain and France, so I forced myself to learn the language. I have done this at each of the clubs abroad I have managed and I will always do this because it is so important. I need to communicate with the players and the media in the language of the country and I need to make the commitment to show I am serious about adapting and fitting in to a new way of life. For me personally it is important to learn the language as a way into the culture.

I expect the same of the players and I see it as a way to measure their professionalism. Of course, if you give me a choice between a player who scores every week or one who learns the language, then I choose the former. Sometimes a player can be useful enough on the pitch not to need words. However, I want both from the player. Making the effort to learn the language enables the player to form better relationships with the other players and staff, and in turn the players and staff appreciate the effort being made to adapt and fit in. Bothering to learn the language is a reliable indicator of the commitment of the player not just to playing the game, but to flourishing in the new environment. This is possibly why English players underperform in foreign leagues. However, while the language was clearly a problem for Gareth Bale in his first year at Madrid, it did not affect his performances and it has obviously improved over time. Maybe the exception that proves the rule.

When I was managing Milan, I would have the players

speak Italian – nothing else – so that we were all speaking the language of the country. Of course, it's more difficult now because you have players from so many different countries and they often like to socialize and speak in their national groups. In France we had Italian players and Argentinian players who spoke Italian together, but at the beginning there was a problem because the French players only spoke French and a natural segregation would form.

You have to address this early in your relationship with the players and get them to understand that cliques are not acceptable. I would manoeuvre them to speak together by having a dinner together and then changing the seating arrangements, sitting people next to others they wouldn't normally socialize with.

The trick is to push the groups together gradually. At Madrid, we put people together at the tables at mealtimes specifically to get them integrated from the beginning. We put new signing Toni Kroos, who is German, close to his countryman Sami Khedira, and then after a certain point put Kroos close to Sergio Ramos and so on. The other thing that I do at clubs is to organize dinners for the players away from the training ground, where they can relax and get to know each other a bit better.

Unfortunately, it can't all be done over mealtime, and a lot of my approach at Paris was spent just gently influencing the players at the training ground, where we spent most of our time. I would subtly split up the groups, mix them up with others. I tried not to force these things but to suggest, to influence – this is the quiet way. I have read the work of the psychologist Robert Cialdini, a good Italian name, on influencing. He talks about the effect of things like consistency, reciprocation and likeability on persuading people. I believe that he has exactly the right ideas.

The importance of players and staff being comfortable with the language is central to quickly understanding the culture of the country and the club. For the business community this is probably even more significant than in football, where player turnover is high and their impact might not be as reliant on the language. If business staff are required to operate in countries with particularly difficult languages for Western people to learn, such as China or an Arab nation, mastering the language, which could take as long as eighteen months, can be inefficient. In such cases there will still be cultural behaviours that can be studied, learned and used to help the person become integrated in that environment.

This same approach is useful in any country if you want to stay and make a success of your time there, as it helps you to understand the culture, the professionalism and how the work ethic is seen in the eyes of the players. These deeper cultural differences are just as important as the language. If you go to work in Spain, for example, you have to follow the culture of Spain. They are used to having lunch at three o'clock, so you have to respect this and you should adapt to it. If I can become assimilated into the culture then the players should be able to do the same.

In England, the professionalism of the British players on the pitch is a given. Of course, you're never sure what happens off the pitch, but on the pitch, they are really professional. We know that not all players are created equal; it is the same with football leagues. Each individual league is made up of different nationalities, and even within those nationalities there are cultural differences. In my career I have found it natural to be immersed in a melting pot of cultures in places such as Paris. In fact, such experiences are a big reason I have chosen to work in so many countries and why I'm looking forward to the next adventure in Bavaria.

I once talked about these cultural differences in an interview and they didn't like it in France. They said that I didn't speak well about their country's football – that I was a racist. I am definitely not racist and the French managers agreed with what I said in the interview. I see differences in the way things are in different countries, different approaches and cultures and management styles. One is not better or worse than the other, but they are different, and you must adapt.

For example, my time in Spain showed me that they like to play football in a certain way and all the teams broadly like to follow that approach. There is more emphasis on possession of the ball. In La Liga, less possession means that you are at the bottom of the league, but that is because everyone plays the same way – everybody accepts the model. If you reject that model you can beat the best teams who play with that model. Bayern Munich, for example, beat

Barça 7–0 over two legs in the Champions League in 2013 with less possession. Leicester City rose to the top of the English Premier League table with some of the worst possession statistics but also one of the highest number of shots of all the teams. This would not be usual in Spain.

In England there is much more aggression and less obsession with possession. English teams and players have a strong fighting mentality. If I had to go to war, I would go with the English, not with the Italians or the French. It is absolutely essential to understand this culture, which is macho like the South Americans, but in a quiet, understated way. Didier Drogba, for example, did not understand, when he first joined Chelsea and was guilty of 'simulation' and exaggerating injuries on the pitch, that a big man simulating injury is not seen as manly in England – it goes against the notion of fair play, and this is a cultural thing. It is different in Spain. John Terry spoke with him and he changed, going on to score lots of goals and become a club legend. Sometimes it is better for this conversation to come from the dressing room leader and not the 'boss'. That player can become the de facto manager for this moment, in the sense that it's more effective when such advice comes from his teammates, peer to peer. It can be more effective and more efficient than if I tell the player myself.

Understanding the culture, having it explained to him by someone steeped in its values, helped Drogba to flourish. This kind of cultural assimilation is fundamental to the success of a multinational, multicultural group of players because it allows relationships between the players and the staff to form and be strengthened. Football is a global business now, with people from all corners of the globe playing at the clubs. The more things the players have in common – the language, observing the cultural values – the better they can communicate and function as a team. Players who don't assimilate become unhappy and might not stay for long. If we think of the club as a family once again, and we look to somewhere like Milan, we can see how long some of the players stayed there. They had integrated efficiently with the culture of the club. Learning the language is the best place to start for a foreign player or member of staff because it communicates one value of the person very clearly: their commitment to becoming part of the club.

Loyalty

It is easy, from the outside looking in, to see football and think that a leader must manage the players and also manage upwards, dealing with expectations from the owner or president, but it is easy to overlook one of the most important relationships at a football club – that between the manager and his support staff. This is where the second aspect of the family comes in, with me and my trusted lieutenants. The support staff should be there to listen, to share ideas, for support and as part of a united front as a management team. Finally, and most importantly, trust between us should be implicit – and loyalty is paramount. It is non-negotiable.

When I hired Giorgio Ciaschini in my first job at Reggiana, we stayed together for ten years at different clubs. A very strong relationship grew up between us, so that he was part of my football family. It should be difficult to break into the 'family', but once in it should be even more difficult to be excluded. As you spend more time in football, working with more people, the family grows, so that you have a bigger and bigger trusted support network around the world of people you can rely upon. It is people who warrant our loyalty – not organizations. With organizations, it's always just business.

Originally, when I was managing in Italy, I had my family, the loyal, trusted people I worked with, and I wanted to take these people with me, from job to job. Many managers do this when they start a job – they replace the staff en masse with their own people. But my time at Chelsea would change my outlook on all of this, and show me that it was possible to forge new loyalties and new ways of working. It would make me more flexible and adaptable in my approach to leading.

When I was having talks with Roman Abramovich and Mike Forde during my courtship with the club, I told them that I wanted to bring my own staff with me, but Abramovich said, 'Look, we have excellent staff and great organization. These are good people working for us. You have to come to the club, see what it's like first and then if you're not happy you can change.' I accepted this – but I added that I wanted to try it for one month. 'If I feel good, great, let's continue,' I said. 'But if I don't feel good we have to change something.'

Chelsea, then, was a first for me, as I didn't bring any of my staff with me from Milanello except for Bruno Demichelis, an Italian psychologist who spoke English. I spent a lot of time thinking things over before agreeing to go to Chelsea. I was not sure – I had always worked with my football family before and I was a little bit worried about the language. Bruno was my safety net and he added value with his experience in the Milan lab. Of course, I would have preferred to bring my family, but it was becoming less common for clubs to allow managers to bring in so many of their own people.

When I arrived I was quickly happy with the staff – there were top-quality people there. Ray Wilkins, who had been working with my predecessor, Guus Hiddink, was helpful because he could speak Italian and therefore be a bridge between me and the players. He was an ex-Milan player, so he was like family already. Ray provided the cultural link you need when entering a new organization. There were also excellent analysts, scientists, nutritionists – all the infrastructure was in place. And then there was Paul Clement.

When I joined I felt that I needed one more trainer, so I spoke to the sporting director, Frank Arnesen, and we agreed to bring in Paul, who was working with the reserves, for fifteen days in the first instance, just to see how he did. After the fifteen days were up, Paul came to me and said, 'Should I go back to the reserves?' I said, 'No, no, no. You stay with me.' Paul became part of my football family. He came with me to Paris and then Madrid, before we went our separate ways when Derby County appointed him as their manager. It was Paul's time to go alone, just like it had been with me and Sacchi before.

When the month's trial with the staff was up, I said, 'OK, we do it this way.'

My experience at Chelsea taught me that you don't necessarily need what you think you want. Working with staff who are already part of the business you are joining can be a huge advantage. Maybe if David Moyes had given the incumbents at Manchester United a chance, things might have been different for him. I thought not having my confidants around me would be a big problem, but it wasn't because I made new ones.

The problem with loyalty is that it can last even when it's damaging. Bringing in tried and trusted lieutenants sounds sensible, but presumably they were also at your side when you were sacked in your previous job. Sometimes it can take external influences to loosen the bonds. I had to leave behind loyal assistants after a successful time in Milan, because of the Chelsea system. But it taught me that you can always make new assistants who are just as loyal – and expand your football family.

The Cultural Bridge

When arriving at a new club in a new country, it is important to have people on the staff who have a cultural link to both the country and the club you're arriving at. As I've mentioned, this was Ray Wilkins for me at Chelsea and at Real Madrid it was Zinedine Zidane. It's so important to settle in quickly, to adapt to the culture and the organization and to know about the players from all levels of the club – and these cultural bridges can help with all of this. At Madrid I had to take five players from the academy and I didn't know anything about these players, but Zidane knew all about them and was able to help me. It didn't hurt that Zidane had a very strong relationship with the president.

I have learned that you cannot rule out the players acting as your support. When I arrived at Paris Saint-Germain I found Claude Makélélé there. He had just retired from playing and our paths never crossed at Chelsea, but I knew of him. He became my cultural link, above all with the French players. He was effectively a key support for me in cultural issues with players and nationalities that were new to me.

In Paris I had carte blanche to appoint my own staff. I brought in the physical trainer I had worked with at Milan. I was able to take Paul Clement and Nick Broad, who was our nutritionist and statistician at Chelsea, and who became our performance manager at Paris Saint-Germain. Sadly, he was killed in a car accident when he was so, so young. He was an amazing man and a big loss.

In my opinion the support staff have the same importance as the players and I try to treat the staff the same as the team. Of course, I have a closer relationship with my staff than with the players, so for this reason it's easier. It's also easier because I don't have to choose between them when match day comes. Effectively, they play every game.

With the staff I look at their character as much as I do with the players or anyone else I work with. I believe that their quality will be more or less the same if they have all the qualifications. For me, again, the most important thing is trust. I need to have trust so that I can feel comfortable to delegate because I want to empower them and have them as involved as possible. I want them to have the freedom to speak with the players and sometimes I use the staff for assistance in speaking with the players myself – directing them in what I want doing. At Real Madrid, Paul Clement was important to help Gareth Bale with his induction into the club – with both the language and the culture – and he was often able to explain things to Bale better than I could.

Every day, together with my staff, we arrange the training sessions. So we speak with each other, we organize together, have ideas together. Speaking with the physical trainer, the doctor or with my assistants can all have an effect on my original ideas. For example, Paul and I might decide that this is the day to have a strength session, but then the physical trainer might say that what we're doing is too much or too soft and that we have to do something different. We then open a discussion and together we'll find the right solution.

Listening, learning, being adaptable – they're all crucial when it comes to integrating effectively into a club's culture. Not only that, but if my experience with the support staff at

Chelsea has taught me anything, it's that you must always be open to new ideas. Leaders cannot afford to stand still, they must always be developing, progressing. This wasn't the only lesson I learned at Chelsea, either.

At Chelsea, as at a lot of English clubs, they integrated the physical side of training with the technical, using data analytics, GPS and other technologies. At Milan we were used to training differently – to separate physical, tactical and technical training sessions. I didn't especially want to change my style of training, but I did so at Chelsea to ensure that there was minimum disruption for the players and I learned to like this way too. Now I'm happy with this style and I don't want to change it, but I am always learning, so, you never know, I may change again. I like to be open to ideas from any source – be it my superiors, my peers, my staff, players or even people outside of football. A culture of improvement is essential to success.

CULTURE: THE QUIET WAY

- Learn the language; if you have insufficient time, study the culture. In other words, demonstrate a willingness to integrate. Insist on that from your staff as well; if you can make the effort, so can they.
- Cliques are unacceptable; eventually, you will have to break them so make it clear from the outset that integration is the only way to win.
- Cultural education can often come better from workmates rather than the boss.
- Managing the support staff is as important as managing the talent. They represent you every day in key moments when you won't be there. Make sure they understand your plans but also the style you want it delivered in.
- You don't always need what you think you want. Change can be liberating; don't resist it just for the sake of it. You will inspire new people very early in the process by making them believe they are still here for a real reason.
- You need to trust in order to delegate.

- Loyalty is at the centre of relationships. It should be hard to break into a family but even harder to be excluded.
- Loyalty is to people, not organizations. For organizations, it's not personal, it's only business.
- Understand the nature of the organization you're in (or plan to join). What's the history and culture? Is it a small business, a family firm or a corporate entity?
- Move towards the culture you now find yourself in. Trust, respect and in some cases time will be granted to you if you demonstrate that you know you are the 'guest' in someone else's world / house.
- Don't get caught in overplaying the value of loyalty in your key lieutenants. Not everyone continues to grow at the pace you need so it is important to access the sustainability of their motivation going forward. People will judge you on how you build a support team to drive performance, not on how loyal you are.

IN THEIR OWN WORDS . . . THE PLAYERS

ZLATAN IBRAHIMOVIĆ ON CARLO

I wrote my memoir *I Am Zlatan* before I met Carlo, so there is no mention of him in the book. If I were to write it all over again, there would be a whole chapter on him describing how, after playing under so many different types of coaches, all different characters, I finally met the best coach ever. It nearly happened before, but I didn't go to AC Milan when he was the coach there; I went to Inter instead. I think he has forgiven me for that by now.

I'd heard a lot about Carlo, but you never know until you meet the person. For me, I don't judge anyone until I meet them and get to know them, and then I give my own opinion. So, from the first day, you get a feeling. The way you approach the person, the way he reacts – I could see immediately that I would like this man. I mean, it takes just a little intelligence to see how a person works and I could see immediately that he was more than just a coach. He is, of course, a brilliant trainer, but for me what counts is the person behind. I believed right from the start that he was the right choice for Paris.

I can speak Italian and English, so immediately we could communicate and get to know each other, and together we started what he called 'the Parisian Project'. Everything was new in the beginning in Paris, totally different to how it is now. The pitches were a state, the team was what it was – it was a completely new project. He had come from Chelsea and I from Milan, two big clubs, to build a club that would *become* big. Although he had already been there six months before me, we started from the beginning.

We'd make jokes about the situation. 'My God, what have we done, where have we come to, what is this place?' we'd ask each other. 'What do we do now, what do we do first, what do we do next?' Every day there was something new to address, which was surprising. It wasn't organized like the big clubs we'd been involved with and you come to expect things to be like that. I mean, even the kit guys – we only had two guys for twenty-five players and we were going away to America. Paris Saint-Germain hadn't won the league for nineteen years and we said, 'OK, we will do this. We will make this a big club.'

Paris was perfect for him and he for Paris, but sometimes when you have other people involved with different ideas things can happen. I know he was very upset to leave and very upset with his friend, Leonardo. Carlo was the first one to come here – which other coach at his level in the game would have come here? It was a big risk. He'd won everything with Milan and Chelsea, but he believed in it – and he convinced other players to come and believe in the project too, and that's not easy.

Let me talk about Carlo the coach. No one gets angry with him, even if they don't play, because he is not just your coach, he's your friend. He treats everybody the same. You think it is just with you because it is so great, so personal, but it's with everybody. He's incredible.

When it comes to being professional, however, and it doesn't go like he wants, he can get angry. We played at Evian, I think, away from home and it was cold. The pitch was terrible and we didn't play well. At half-time, you always know when something is going on because that one eyebrow goes up. As I sat down I thought, 'Now he's angry.' Carlo was speaking to us and there was a box in front of him and from nowhere he kicked it and it flew through the air and hit me on the head. 'Jesus,' I thought, 'now he's really angry.' I had never seen him like this before. When he gets angry, he gets angry – but only out of sight. Only in the dressing room. For him, what is most important is the respect. He gives you respect and he expects it in return. If you don't respect him, then we have a problem, but the thing is that you cannot help but have great respect for him – it's impossible not to.

I saw this with all the players, which is unusual. In every team I've played for you see that, when players don't make the team, they get annoyed with the coach, but with Carlo it didn't happen. And if somebody were to get close to that point, I would say to them, 'Believe me, you have a coach who only wants good things for you, even if you don't play as much as you'd like. He cares for you and you will notice the difference when you have another coach.' This is what everybody said when we lost him at Paris, and when he changed things at Real Madrid, the players there said that it was like they'd hoped football could be.

I say Carlo is the best and I have worked with the best. To compare them, let me take you through them one by one. Mourinho is the disciplinarian. Everything with him is a mind game – he likes to manipulate. Such tricks were new for me – all the time doing one thing to get another thing, all the time triggering me. I like these games and it worked for me; I became top scorer under him and we won the league. As long as it works and as long as we win, it's all good with me.

The way Mourinho prepared for games was also new to me. I would get pumped up, believing the story he would feed us. I went through a lot of adrenaline when I played for him. It was like nothing was ever good enough. He gave and he took. José

Mourinho knows how to treat a footballer, but Carlo knows how to treat a person.

After Mourinho I went to Pep Guardiola, the big brain in football. He had all these solutions for every team we played against, knowing exactly what we needed to do to win, exactly how he wanted it achieved. We could be winning 2–0 at half-time, but he would say, 'We're not finished here – we continue. I want three, four, five, six, seven.' He was like a machine.

As a person, however, he was something else. I told you that I don't judge a person if I don't know them, and I base these opinions on what I went through with him. As a coach, he's fantastic, but as a person, we didn't see eye to eye on many things. I wrote about our problems in my own book. It was like a school and we, the players, were the schoolboys. This type of environment does not suit me.

Even after Guardiola, when they lost so badly to Bayern Munich, 7–0, in the Champions League, nothing changed. Because they'd had such success for the ten years before that game they treated it as a one-off. They are so strong and confident that they believe in themselves and just follow the system all the time. This works for them but not so good for me.

Barça have always had a world-class team, but under

Guardiola the system stayed the same. Outside of this system, and outside of his huge footballing brain, I cannot agree that Guardiola is the same quality as Carlo.

So, later, after I have had this experience with Guardiola, I meet Carlo. I get a complete person *and* a coach. Often with a coach the game is all we have in common, but with Carlo, when I have a problem at home I can talk to him; when I need advice I can talk to him – whatever it was, I knew I could lean on him. But it wasn't only me – it was the same for the whole group. He is who he is with everybody.

I remember the game against Porto in the Champions League, because there was a lot of pressure. It was win or lose his job. I felt for him because we had been winning everything, and then because we had just lost, suddenly it was chaos. Quietly, he said that the competition was not finished. 'You do not win the trophies now,' Carlo said. 'You win them in the end of the season.' But there was still chaos everywhere because a small club doesn't know how to handle setbacks when they arrive. A big club knows that bad times are inevitable and they know how to handle them because they've been through it. However, no matter how much chaos there was, Carlo handled it. He knew what he needed to do because of his experience. The chaos was never allowed to reach the team.

The training ground was small, so we could hear the noise that would go on at the club, but Carlo would never agree with the owners if they criticized the players. He would always protect us. He would say that the players had done everything he had asked of us.

He protected the team in many ways. If someone was late to training because they had been out the night before, he would call them into his office and ask what had happened. He would listen and then say, 'Don't do this again. This is between me and you, but don't repeat this mistake. Be professional.' He had a sense of humour with it too, when it was appropriate, and he might add, 'Next time you invite me along.'

Because he was like this, sometimes it was hard to tell if he was really angry or just playing angry. Even when he kicked the box and hit me in the head with it, I wasn't sure – nobody had done anything like that to me before – but, as it was Carlo, and I looked at him and saw that the eyebrow was up, I knew it was serious, so I just put my head down. One day he was wearing a beautiful Italian suit and he went crazy, screaming at everybody and then swearing in Italian. Nobody knew what the problem was so we all just sat in silence. The next day, it was hugs. He would say sorry for being angry.

One day in training I approached him and said, 'Coach, Coach,

I need to talk to you.' It was like he was pretending he didn't hear me, so I prodded him with my pointed finger and said, 'Coach.' From nowhere he turned to me with a very serious face and said, 'Never put a finger on me.' I was in shock. 'Are you serious?' I asked. 'Yes, I'm serious – never put a finger on me.' Then two seconds later he started to laugh. I said, 'Carlo, don't surprise me like this, because I don't recognize you.' He has that glint in his eye. He has the feeling for every person.

The day after the game he would make it a point to talk to everybody. He would say if somebody had a bad game and talk to them about it. Before we played away against Barcelona in the quarter-final of the Champions League, everybody was pumped. Carlo said, 'Ibra, I need to talk to you.' When he speaks in a certain serious tone you know that it's important. We sat down and he looked uncomfortable when he said, 'I've been thinking about this for a long time. We will do things differently in this game. I've decided to put you on the bench.'

'What?' I said.

'It is a tactical trick we will play,' he said. 'When everybody is tired in the last twenty minutes, you will come on.' I was devastated, but I also wanted him to know that I could be professional about it. 'OK,' I said.

'I'm joking with you,' he said, smiling. 'Go have your lunch.' All the tension disappeared after that. He could really help you relax before a big game.

In another game Carlo explained his tactics: 'We will park the bus in front of goal and Ibra in front of the bus. Everybody is expecting us to play tika-taka football, but I say we're here to win.' He will always do what needs to be done to win the game.

Mourinho is like this too. He was always well informed about opponents, going through their every weakness and every quality and then the way he wanted the game to be. If he wanted to kill the game, he'd kill the game; if he wanted the game to be open, it would be open. For Mourinho, it was all about winning. In Italy, where I played for him, it's more important not to concede a goal than to score a goal, and Mourinho adapts very well to every country. He knows that winning is the only thing, though it seems that his third season at clubs often presents a problem for him. In Madrid it was perfect for Carlo to come after Mourinho – he's the only one that could succeed with a team after Mourinho. The players need the calm after the fighting.

I hear that the president at Madrid complained that some of the players began to take advantage of Carlo's good nature. This is wrong. Maybe the president was jealous because he didn't have the same relationship with the players that Carlo did. I don't understand this criticism.

I understand how people who don't know what it is like to be in a high-performance team can mistake a good relationship for weakness, but it is, in fact, the opposite. The atmosphere must be comfortable for the players. I remember when we were out for dinner at an Italian restaurant, a group of seven or eight of us from the team. It was quite late, about eleven o'clock, and someone suggested calling Carlo. Some of the guys said that he would not even answer, others thought he wouldn't expect us to be out so late, but we called him anyway. Ten minutes later he joined us, had a drink, chatted and joked with us and then he left after one hour. Tell me any other coach that would have done this. Who else but Carlo has such confidence?

When you have a person who is comfortable within these kind of limits, you would do everything for him. The confidence he gives you and the confidence he gets in return – you would kill for him. In football, to take orders from the general you have to believe in him.

He is not afraid to speak to individuals in front of the group. There were many situations when he criticized me in front of everybody. He would make a point of criticizing the big player – the towers of the team – to show that nobody is too important to be above criticism.

The sign of a big player is that they're able to accept this. The smaller players, they feel that they need to defend themselves – they do not yet have the confidence to admit their faults. But if they see the towers of the team accepting their mistakes, they will be more able to do the same – and this is the only way to learn. Carlo would say to the team, 'We conceded a goal – what happened there?' The big players would say, 'My fault.' Then it's done. He does it this way because it gives the responsibility to the big players. He needs to trust them.

There was a situation with two players in the same position, each with equal quality. They were playing alternate matches, so, out of curiosity, I asked Carlo, 'How are you playing this game with them?' He said, 'I go to the first one and tell him he will be my right-back. Then I go to the other one and say exactly the same thing. So now it's up to them who will do it on the pitch.' You never know if he is joking, of course, but I think he is always on the edge with his methods, which the confidence and respect he's built up allow him to use. He has this feeling about things – either you have it or you don't.

Carlo's way of working, the training sessions and the like, is pretty old school and very Italian. Tactics are important for him. I've played in Italy and I know how it works in Italy – always very tactical the day before the game. Carlo would have us out on the training pitch for a tactical brief, which isn't always easy as a player – you need to be stimulated all the time instead of standing still and shivering in the cold, but he believed strongly in it. Whichever way he approached the training, the coaching was successful. Don't forget he was a football player once, who won trophies. Not many coaches have done this; he has it all in his locker, which he can pull out at any time.

I'm just happy and lucky that I worked with him and I'm sorry that it didn't last longer. When I speak to him now he says, 'Ibra, where do you want to go next? Which team?' I tell him that if he's at a team I don't need to think about it, I'll be there. 'Anywhere but Russia.'

When we played away to Lyon towards the end of the season, we knew that, if we won, we would be champions. I remember before the game, his eyebrow was already up in the morning because he was nervous. I had not seen this before. I said to him, 'Carlo, do you believe in God?'

'Yes,' he replied. So I said, 'That's good, because you can believe in me.' The eyebrow went up even more. 'Ibra, you're such a bastard . . .' he said, and after that we won and were champions.

He helped me to mature both as a player and as a man. At the beginning I was like a lion, on and off the pitch. I would throw things when we were losing. Paris Saint-Germain was too relaxed for me, but Carlo used this. If the game had gone maybe ten minutes with nothing happening, he would call to me on the pitch, 'Ibra – time to wake up the team.'

Carlo saw me as the leader. I think being a leader isn't something you choose – it's something you become. Either you're a leader or you're not. When I arrived in Paris Carlo said, 'You will be my captain,' and it is the only thing I have refused with Carlo. I said, 'Carlo, I don't know how long I will stay here, because I come, I do my job and I leave. A captain should be just like you – a person for this project for a long time.'

He tried to persuade me, but I told him to make Thiago Silva captain. I think that he still sees me as a leader, with or without the armband. Either you are or you are not. Having the armband doesn't mean that you are a real captain, though Thiago Silva is both the captain *and* a leader. I hope I help him in that.

Carlo is a natural leader. His style isn't ostentatious – it's quiet. He is not pretending; there's nothing false about it. You have many out there whose style is to pretend, to show off, but in the end they will lose – people will see through them. Carlo is always true to himself. If he weren't, I would not say these words about him. I am not a man to mince my words.

The club that Paris Saint-Germain is today is not thanks to the people coming in now, it's thanks to Carlo, who was here at the beginning. It's the guys at the start, who had all that hard work to do, who people should be saying thanks to, not the people here dancing and enjoying it now that everything is nice. When he left, I was not sure I wanted to stay, because I had a very good relationship with him. Even if we hadn't won the league, I would still believe in him. I believe he was the right person for this project, but not for two years. *Ten* years would have been right and that was his vision too.

He believed in it so much, and he believed too that he was the right person to bring it to fruition. I was very sorry when he left, both for professional and personal reasons. He called me and explained everything and I said, 'I don't want you to leave – maybe this will be my last year as a football player and I would like to spend it under you as a coach.' He said, 'No, we go our separate ways. I have already chosen Real Madrid because it has become bad for me here at PSG.' I knew Real Madrid's players would be happy because I knew what they were getting, just as I knew what we had lost.

'From now on, you don't call me Coach,' he said to me. We all called him Coach or Mister Ancelotti. 'This is an order,' he continued. 'You don't call me Mister any more – you call me by my name, because I consider you a friend. Listen to what I'm saying because you will offend me if you call me Mister.'

I've never had a relationship with a coach like I had with him. I know how it is in football. We are friends today, my teammates and I, but if I leave the team next year, how many will I speak to? I don't know. You never know, because these are football friends, workmates. How many do you keep close to in any walk of life? I have Maxwell, my friend at the club who I will probably keep in touch with for the rest of my life, and also there is Carlo. I still talk to him today – he is my friend.

3. Hierarchy

Managing Up

The arrangements between the ultimate boss – the owner or president of the club – and the governance and management structure that sits below can be labyrinthine. These complex structures are not necessary, because football clubs aren't massive businesses. In financial terms they are mid-sized at best. What complicates things is that, unlike in more regular businesses where roles are marked out and the end product less readily open to constant feedback, everyone involved is so passionate about football. *Everyone* has an opinion. It is said that in academia the arguments are so fierce because the issues are so trivial; it is the same in football.

In my mind the distinction between the boss – for me, this is the president – and what I call the general director – in business terms, the CEO, but it comes with various names in football – is an important one to make. After this chapter, my old boss at Milan, general director Adriano Galliani, speaks eloquently about how he sees the demarcation of duties, but for me, my job remains to try to handle them all in a calm, influential and pragmatic style. 'Managing up' is a reality in all businesses.

People ask how I dealt with Silvio Berlusconi at Milan, Roman Abramovich at Chelsea, Florentino Pérez at Real Madrid or Nasser Al-Khelaifi at Paris Saint-Germain. I'll tell you: For me, it's not so important. I don't spend a lot of time with the president. Mostly I spend time with the general director and it is he who spends time with the president. Basically, we do the same jobs but at different levels. He tries to protect me from what my friend Alessandro Nesta calls the 'presidential noise' and in turn I try to protect the players from anything from above that might distract them. I can't control the direction of the president; I can only hope to influence him, and the best way to do that is by winning. Of course, I understand that if he is happy, I am happy, and if he's not happy, then I do not have a job and I cannot protect the players.

With Berlusconi I learned, very quickly, that since he owned AC Milan, my job was to please Berlusconi. The tradition at Milan is to play an attractive style of football – which is different from Juventus, where the most important thing is to win. So, I built a team for Berlusconi to enjoy. I built an attacking team with Pirlo, Seedorf, Rui Costa, Kaká and Shevchenko all playing at the same time. I learned that no system is more important than the club president. If Berlusconi wants to come in the dressing room to tell his jokes, then I have to understand that it is his dressing room. I even allowed him into the dressing room before we played Juventus in the Champions League final in 2003. He's the boss, so he can even listen to the team talk if he wants.

Everyone thinks that Berlusconi pushed me, but this is not really true. He was affectionate. He would actually push me when we were winning, but when things were going wrong he would support me. When we were doing well, he would tell me, 'No, we have to play with this striker. We have to play with more attacking football. This is not my opinion – I am *telling you* that this is what I want.'

I would reply, 'We have two strikers. Shevchenko in the side, we have also Kaká playing with him.' 'No,' he would say. 'Kaká's not a striker, Kaká is a midfielder.' It was just to put his two cents' worth in when everything was going well. Rumour had it that he tried to pick the team by sending me team sheets before games. This is simply not true. The teams were always my teams. Sometimes, after a game when we had won, he liked to add his opinion and would tell me who and how he would have played, but it was always *after* the game and after we had won.

Ultimately, you could say my role at any club is to keep the president happy. How do I do that? I do not go to the president, but I have to be ready to answer any questions that he asks me when he comes to me. My time at Chelsea certainly taught me the importance of this. My regular meetings are with the general director, who reports back to the president, and we meet usually once a week, but it often isn't scheduled and it differs at every club – there are no set rules. At Paris Saint-Germain I would meet every day with Leonardo, but at Madrid and Chelsea it was different.

That was part of why I was so surprised and disappointed in Paris when I was given the ultimatum from the president and Leonardo to win the next game against Porto or be fired. To come from the president, of course, this happens. But I had been meeting with Leonardo every day, explaining the training, the injury situation, our planned tactics, strategies. For him to say out of nowhere 'win this next game', when we'd already qualified, it made no sense to me. We'd been talking every day.

So, the general director is the conduit between the president and me, passing on my messages to the president and vice versa. Naturally, it is very important for me to have a good relationship with the general director, as we spend a lot of time together and he can influence how the president sees me. Another useful function of the general director is to act as a buffer between the president and me. When either of us might become angry or annoyed, it is the general director who can act as peacemaker. Galliani played this role a lot at Milan.

At Chelsea it was difficult at first because the chief executive, Peter Kenyon, left shortly after I arrived. In that first year it was the sporting director, Frank Arnesen, who played this role. There was still a chairman and other board members and, of course, the owner was always very interested in what was happening, which is as it should be. But then Arnesen left and there was a vacuum between me and the owner. There was no conduit, no buffer, so the conversations with him became unpredictable and I wasn't always prepared for them. Perhaps this would have been fine as a temporary measure, but the Arnesen role was not replaced and there was confusion about the reporting structure. It wasn't that there was nobody doing that job – it was that everybody was trying to do it.

At my other clubs this hierarchy was always very clear. At Milan there was Galliani; at Juventus there was Luciano Moggi, of the infamous Calciopoli scandal which saw Juventus stripped of two Scudettos and demoted a division; at Paris Saint-Germain there was Leonardo, of course; and at Real Madrid there was José Ángel Sánchez, who is the ultimate politician and survivor at the club. He was hired by Pérez but then worked for Ramón Calderón when he became president of the club and then went back to working for Pérez in his second term, while I was at Madrid. He is a powerful lieutenant for Pérez.

This kind of structure isn't normal for English clubs, although I understand that it is becoming more so. Tradition fights against it, but British managers who resist it are putting themselves under unnecessary pressure to be all things at once to the club. Football clubs are now too big a business for one person to manage.

It's important that the manager sometimes *doesn't* speak about certain things and isn't responsible for every detail. With the players, for example, it is not the best idea for the manager to always be the one to speak with them about disciplinary matters. Suppose one player arrives back late after the winter break or for preseason. The player must be fined, but should the manager have to be the one to take that responsibility, which might cause bad blood and resentment from the player? No – it surely has to be the club, so that the manager can be distanced from the decision and continue to do his job without any bad feeling.

At Madrid, we had some players who went out partying until four o'clock in the morning. I could say to them, 'What are you doing? You know this isn't right.' But it is up to the club to fine them or suspend them – it doesn't have to be the manager. This is important, this balancing of responsibilities between player, coach and club, because damage can be done to the relationship between the coach and player if it is not handled well.

When the club behaves correctly and fairly with all players, with no favouritism, it can only add to the manager's authority. The manager has power only if the players see that the club always protects the manager against the players and their agents. When the players see that the club doesn't protect the manager, that's often it for them – they're dead. However, sometimes when the club does not back the manager it can actually create a stronger bond with the players if the relationships have been built well enough. At Paris Saint-Germain the players knew the situation between me and the club because I had told them about the 'win or go' conversation with Leonardo and the president, and this did indeed make the relationship between us even stronger.

Of course, it could have weakened me if the players had taken it a different way, but we already had built the right spirit of unity to survive it. Under normal circumstances, I would usually try to keep this type of 'presidential noise' away from them, but I felt I had no choice at the time. It helped galvanize us as a team and we won the next game.

At Madrid we had a different kind of noise and it did adversely affect what happened on the pitch. I've already mentioned the saga of the medical statistics which said we had a low number of training hours. The president latched on to the stats and said that we were not working hard enough. I tried to explain to him that it wasn't the *amount* of training but rather the *intensity* that was important; we could train three hours slowly, but it's better to train thirty minutes fast and hard. He wouldn't listen. If the president had waited he would have seen, when the blood-test results arrived twenty-one days later, that we actually needed to ease off a little.

Methods in football can look bad to those not embedded in the game itself – even to presidents and general directors. When you lose a game and then you have a day off afterwards, many people ask, 'What are you doing?' Their reaction is to get the players in and push them after a bad result, but this is wrong. The reverse is true. When you lose, of course you have to analyse what went wrong and how to address it next time, but you have to put that game behind you. You have to try to forget the defeat as soon as possible so you're in the right frame of mind for the next game. It is at times like this that the president and the press will begin to say, 'You're too weak, you're too nice. The players aren't performing so you have to show them the whip.' Every time we lose, that's what they say. The same was true at Milan, Chelsea and Paris Saint-Germain, as well as Real Madrid. It is normal in football and part of the deal you must make with yourself before you take the job. You have to let it wash over you and be confident in your own approach.

My opinion is that players do their best when they are comfortable, not when they are uncomfortable. I have a story I like to tell about this. Two people have a horse each and they have to get their animal to jump a fence. The first owner stands behind the horse and uses a whip to force the horse and the horse jumps the fence. The second owner stands in front of the fence with carrots in his hand to invite the horse over and his horse jumps over it too. They both jumped the fence this time, but if you use the whip, sometimes the horse will kick back instead of jumping. That's the problem.

When I talk of players being comfortable, I do not mean in their playing – I mean in their minds. They must understand that I am always trying to make them and the team better. The comfort is in the trust built by the relationship. In the end, everyone has to respect the rules and that enables a friendly relationship to exist, even if my decision is that the player has to go on the bench. On one such occasion, when I left a player out of the team, he said to me, 'But we are friends.'

'Yes, of course we're friends,' I explained, 'and for that reason you can see why you don't play – because we're friends and I can be honest with you. You must be treated the same as any other player.'

Sometimes presidents question whether, when I have developed a strong relationship with players, I give them more game time than their form demands. I do my very best for this not to be the case because it would upset the team ethic, but maybe – and it is only a maybe – I can be too patient with players who have served the team well and have been loyal to me.

I was asked this about Sergio Ramos, when he'd had some bad games for Madrid but was still playing. My answer was quite simple. Ramos was the most important player in the squad. He was a leader, the player with the most personality, the most character. Of course, sometimes he made mistakes, but I definitely did not pick him more than I should have done because of my relationship with him. He was playing because he was so important to the team. You must look back in these situations, take in the bigger picture. We lost games when Ramos was injured. We put in younger players but they were not adequate replacements.

When it came to changing his position, playing him in midfield for a while to help the team in my second season, Ramos was worried because it was so new for him, but he agreed and did as I asked because he trusted me. If I hadn't built such a relationship with him he might have been reluctant to play in midfield. In my first year at the club I played him at right back for a game, but we hadn't yet built this relationship – he didn't know me well. He told me after the game, 'That's the last time I play right back.' But the next year was different. So, when he didn't play that well in a match in his new and unfamiliar position in midfield, he was only one among others in the team that didn't play well, so why, then, would I single him out? He was doing what I had asked for the good of the team and it is up to me to protect him for this. This is my view of managing up – to protect the players and to manage expectations. The first is easy, it is natural, but the second is very hard.

In football, especially at the top clubs, the expectation is always there, whether it's to deliver 'La Décima', as it was for me at Madrid, to provide a certain style of play, as at Milan, or to win a specific game. It never stops. The general director will always keep me informed of the expectations from above and I will always do my best to manage these so that they do not have a negative impact on the players.

My way, as in all things, is to be constantly building relationships, to have a working understanding with the conduit to the president, the general director, and to have the confidence of the players. I invest heavily in building relationships around the club, while being pragmatic about knowing where the ultimate power lies. If the president believes he is being 'managed', then I have failed in that relationship.

HIERARCHY: THE QUIET WAY

- Manage expectations from above to protect those you lead from the 'presidential noise'.
- Never be afraid to delegate; nobody's good enough to do everything.
- Don't be perceived as 'managing' relationships above you. Owners and presidents have egos; treat those egos carefully.
- Don't play favourites – this is a business.
- The quickest and most effective way to keep your owner or board happy is to win. To win you need to nurture and build the best relationship with your talent. The real relationship with your board will be built on this foundation.
- Take your owner on the journey with you. Make them understand they are a part of the story. Overcommunicate on the key issues that drive success and manage the 'noise' they can create around the other areas.

IN THEIR OWN WORDS . . . THE BOSS

ADRIANO GALLIANI ON CARLO

I have been at AC Milan for thirty years. I am the CEO at the club and I was Carlo Ancelotti's boss for eight years. It is hard to explain the role of CEO at a big football club, but this is how I see it. The CEO of a football company should *industrialize* the game of football.

As a game, football has existed for a long time, but if somebody didn't come along and industrialize it, football would have remained a game played by boys on a beach or a field. They started to introduce rules – offsides and the like – and coaches started to teach people how to play the game properly. Then somebody started to plan how this game could become a serious business. Football starts with people going to stadiums, then, thanks to sponsorship and TV money, it becomes a multimillion-dollar phenomenon – a global industry. The chief of a football company, what can he do? He industrializes the game for his company.

The football industry is similar to the American movie

business. A football match lasts ninety minutes, like a film, and it's exploited in the same way. The stadium is the movie theatre; its exploitation is in television and home viewing, exactly like in the cinema industry. You can spend a lot of money producing bad films and games, or less money and get successful films and games. You can't guarantee it. The roles are the same as in the movies: the players are the actors, the coach is the director and the president or CEO is the producer. Carlo was my director at Milan.

I first met Carlo Ancelotti in August 1987. The club had appointed a new coach, Arrigo Sacchi, who arrived in Milan the month before. In Italy it is the coach who trains and proposes what he needs for the team and it is the CEO or president who decides whom to buy and how much to pay and does the negotiation, because they are the people who put the money in. In England I understand the role is different and that the manager is both a coach and the person who buys and sells players.

So, let's begin at the beginning because it's a nice story. When Sacchi needed a new midfielder and asked for Ancelotti, Silvio Berlusconi and I were worried because he had suffered serious injuries to his knee, but we decided to go for him all the same. We started courting Roma, whose president, Dino Viola, didn't want to sell him at the opening of the transfer market, but on the very last day said yes. I rushed to Rome on the evening before the last day and, in order to stop the press getting wind of it before we could unveil it all, we had booked a hotel room to have the meeting. Carlo got there at about eight o'clock, took the first room key and went up, and a little while later I arrived and asked for my room key at reception. The hotel receptionist gave me a funny look, if you understand what I mean, and handed me the key.

Carlo and I got along very well immediately – we talked about football and many things besides. I invited him for dinner at the home of my then fiancée, who is from Rome. The following day he underwent our medical examinations and our doctor expressed misgivings about the knee and advised us not to buy him. Sacchi pressed Berlusconi and me and we decided to buy him anyway, for about five or six billion lire, which was no little amount for a player who was already twenty-eight and had big problems with his knee. Because the market was closing at 7 p.m., we had to rush the contracts in our private jet to the league headquarters. This was thirty years ago, remember, before electronic devices. In those days it was the jet then motor-cycle courier to register the paper contract at the league. So began Ancelotti's five-year adventure in Milan as a player.

He spent his first four years with Sacchi as his coach and the last under Fabio Capello. It was a splendid adventure. We won the 1987–88 league championship in his first year, then we won two European Cups, in 1989 and 1990. In 1991–92 we won the championship again and in the last match, against Verona, Carlo scored two goals. Altogether in that period we won two league championships, two Champions Leagues, two Super Cups, two Intercontinental Cups (the 'world championship' for clubs) . . . a lot of trophies. It was incredible.

When he hurt his knee again, at the age of thirty-three, he decided to quit as a player. And what happens? The never-ending story continues because Arrigo Sacchi, who had left Milan in 1991 to become the coach of the national team, summons Carlo to be his assistant at the 1994 World Cup. With these two Milan old boys at the helm and seven or eight Milan players as regulars in the team, Italy got to the final against Brazil, where they lost on penalties.

In 1995 he went to coach Reggiana and won the second division championship, then moved to Parma, a medium-sized club, where he had two very good seasons, finishing second in one of them. I always watched his progress and stayed in contact, even when he started coaching our main rivals in 1999. The Juventus fans didn't love Carlo because he had been a player for Roma and, most importantly, for Milan. When he arrived at the San Siro with his Juventus team in 2000, the Milan fans applauded Ancelotti, while the Juventus fans whistled him.

Juventus is a big club. He had done very well with Parma so it was natural he would go there. Milan already had a successful coach at this time, in the form of Alberto Zaccheroni, who won the championship in his first year and was with us for three years. At that moment Milan didn't need another coach. But it is natural that coaches move on. All over the world coaches move. Marcello Lippi, an extraordinary coach, was doing well at Juventus before Ancelotti, but sometimes you need a change. Changing coaches is in the life of a club – it's normal.

Ancelotti's Juventus twice finished in second place in the league, when they could have won it. He *almost* won it and that was when Ancelotti got the reputation for being a good loser – a nearly man. Being the runner-up may be OK at some clubs, but not at Juventus, and the club dismissed him.

So, in the summer of 2001 he was a coach with a contract and a salary from Juventus, but he wasn't coaching. We hired a Turkish coach at Milan, Fatih Terim, who stayed for six matches and then, the night we lost to Torino, we dismissed him. Carlo had always stayed in our hearts – it is a relationship that will never be broken – so I immediately called him. I knew he planned to sign for Calisto Tanzi, president of Parma, but I wasn't sure if he already had. 'Not yet,' he told me, 'but what can I do? I have already given my word to Tanzi.'

'Do not sign,' I said. 'I'm coming.' I dashed to Ancelotti's home where I played on his affection for Milan, on his relationship with the club. Carlo said yes and his second adventure at Milan began.

At Ancelotti's home we had Lambrusco wine – not the kind they drink in England, but *real* Italian Lambrusco – culatello, prosciutto crudo and parmigiano. At Ancelotti's home you always eat well. He gets his ingredients from Parma which is, for Carlo, the European food capital. Last time I was with him in Madrid, he cooked, preparing everything personally, and it was delicious.

I digress. Let's go back, to Carlo joining the club. He steadies the ship and we climb the table, getting to fourth position and into the next season's Champions League. In this competition in 2003 we reach the semi-finals along with two other Italian clubs, Juventus and our local rivals Inter. Three out of the four semi-finalists Italian – a success that is unlikely to happen again anytime soon. We are drawn against Inter and we eliminate them, while Juventus beat Real Madrid to reach the final.

Then the most beautiful thing in the world happens, and it will stay engraved in Milan fans' hearts for ever. We beat Juventus on penalties to win the Champions League under Carlo in Manchester. Three days later, we win the Coppa Italia against Roma. The Champions League *and* the Coppa Italia in a matter of days. Fantastic!

Our adventure with Carlo goes on. We win the European Super Cup in 2003, the Scudetto in 2004 – a marvellous time for the club. In 2005 we finish second in the league and reach the Champions League final again, but we lose in Istanbul against Liverpool. In 2007 we would have a repeat of this final and win this time. Milan were first in the European rankings, ahead of Real Madrid and Barcelona, in July 2007.

Those eight years with Carlo were Milan's most beautiful period. As always, there were victories and defeats, but many more victories. We won eight trophies: an Italian championship, a Coppa Italia, a Supercoppa Italia, two Champions Leagues, two European Super Cups and a Club World Cup. If you add this to the trophies he won as a player, Carlo can boast an unbelievable curriculum vitae. Together with Pep Guardiola of Barcelona and Miguel Muñoz of Real Madrid, Carlo is one of only three people in the world to have won the Champions League as a player and a coach with the same club. In the end, something magical and marvellous happened.

I am always asked if there were recriminations after the Istanbul final, but that was not the case. We supported Carlo. Our reaction was of great sorrow, but in Istanbul Milan had played marvellously during the first half and the whole of the second except for those six minutes during which we conceded three goals. We should have won. In the 120th minute Shevchenko was stopped by a miraculous save by Jerzy Dudek. Destiny. Milan won two years later in Athens but played much worse.

During those five beautiful years we reached three Champions League finals, one semi-final and a quarter-final, which was incredible. Nobody could come close to us during that period – not Barcelona, nor Bayern, nor Real.

I don't believe there exists a magic formula about how a coach should be. Carlo is a great motivator and he has his own way to manage his players, just as Mourinho has his and Guardiola his. Ultimately, results do speak for a coach. Each of us has his own way. With children, for example, there are hard parents, soft parents, those who use the stick and those who use the carrot. In the end the results say if you were right or wrong, and Ancelotti's history speaks of the greatest results. He won in Italy, in England with Chelsea he won the Premier League, he won Ligue 1 in France and, with Real Madrid, who had been winning nothing for centuries, he won the Champions League.

Despite being this multinational, multicultural leader, Carlo has never betrayed his roots or abandoned his way of being. He has remained the boy from Parma. Carlo has this great capacity for enlivening the atmosphere where he works. He spreads serenity because he is a serene man.

In life people must be accepted for what they are. You cannot demand someone to spread serenity, or to be Arnold Schwarzenegger, if these things are not of themselves. Carlo is made like that. It's useless for me to say that he should be harder or stricter, or he should be this or that, because, if he were so, he would lose some of his other qualities.

One of my favourite episodes was when I attended the last training session on the evening before the Champions League final against Liverpool in Athens in 2007. Pippo Inzaghi, our centre forward, was completely out of sync – he was barely able to trap the ball. We had another strong centre forward, Alberto Gilardino, who had scored in the semi-final against Manchester United. As I was standing at Ancelotti's side on the field watching Inzaghi miss every single ball, I said to him: 'Why don't we let Gilardino play? He looks to be in much better shape than Inzaghi.' Carlo simply said: 'Inzaghi is a strange animal. Maybe tomorrow will be his night.' Inzaghi scored two goals in the final.

Any other coach, watching how Gilardino was playing and had performed in the semi-final and then looking how Inzaghi was playing, would have chosen Gilardino. It wasn't as if Gilardino was an untried player: he was a valuable asset. Carlo had agreed with me that Inzaghi wasn't doing well, but he just had a feeling. He has this feeling for the game. He said to me afterwards, 'After thirty years I've developed an eye for this and I've learned to trust it.'

My job is to give my opinion, but I always respect the coach and his decision, and the final decision always belongs to the coach. On the field we were like two friends and I was able to give my opinion without it being considered any imposition of my will.

As with all things in life, there comes a natural break point. I believe that a coach, as excellent as he can be, cannot remain at the same club for ever. It's inescapable and unavoidable that he should change. Eight years had gone by and we still had a contract for one year – it was due to expire in 2010, not 2009. Carlo was very honest and upfront and told us that Chelsea wanted him. Chelsea had become a very big club under Roman Abramovich, with lots of money and potential. Carlo very clearly and correctly had told Chelsea that the decision had to be made by

Milan. Had we said no, he wouldn't have gone. He would have honoured his promise, his contract – this is Carlo's way. He had done the same once before, when Madrid came for him and he didn't go.

Berlusconi and I discussed it many times and in the end decided that a change was best for both parties. In football everything has an end, and so after eight years we let him go to experience a new adventure. He very much wanted to go to England and it was a consensual separation. There was no trauma. We simply split amicably, with each of us going our own way, but still retaining our bond. Nowadays, when a coach is still under contract, clubs will ask for money as compensation to let them go. It's like when you buy a player – if you want him, you must pay for him. We didn't ask Chelsea for a penny. He was free to go.

I spent five days in Madrid with Carlo as soon as I heard that Real Madrid had sacked him. I wanted to convince him to come back to Milan. Berlusconi and I wanted to bring him home. We courted him, but in the end it was not to be. He said no because he had to undergo an operation on his neck. I believe that last summer, if it wasn't for the operation, he might have come to Milan. Perhaps he was worried about returning. They say 'Never go back' and I can understand this. Thirteen years with Milan is a lot. It's difficult to go back after so long as a player and a coach – and with such a strong relationship between us. This friendship with Carlo has kept going for thirty years.

4. Talent

The players are, of course, the most important part of any football club. Without the players, there is no football, no fans – nothing. It's as true in the entertainment industry – without the talent there is no show – as it is in business. Without the core staff to make it all happen, where is the business? Managing the talent, then, is at the heart of the leadership challenge in any organization. Key to this are the crucial elements of the talent cycle – recruitment, onboarding, development and succession – that apply to the players. And in turn I am aware that I am part of a talent cycle for those above me, the general director and president, that they will address also.

My starting point is that players and staff are first and foremost people – they are not defined by their roles, their positions, or their jobs. When I first meet a player at a new club I might ask them: 'Who are you?' They may reply: 'I'm a player, I'm a great attacking midfielder.' But I might then tell them: 'No. You're [their name]. You're a man who plays football. You're brilliant at it, world class, but it doesn't define you.' I try to see the full person and to help them see themselves in a broader way.

Recruitment

In football, as in business, there are a wide variety of pressures – commercial, cultural, political – that must be accommodated when recruiting top-level talent in a highly competitive market. In business they talk about the 'war for talent' and this is also true of football – there has always been a war. As with all wars, you have to pick your battles, match your ambition to your resources, build strategic allegiances and, most importantly, be smarter than the other guy.

My role in recruitment is not a normal one for a business, but it is how it is done at a football club, particularly in mainland Europe. The negotiations are usually the responsibility of the general manager, though often a player will want to speak with the new manager before deciding whether to join the team. Sometimes these little personal touches can make all the difference in swaying an undecided player. I have spoken with almost every new player who has signed with my team prior to them making their decision, at the behest sometimes of the club, sometimes of the player's agent and sometimes of the player himself.

The special players have to satisfy themselves that the move is right for them. One example is David Beckham. He is smart enough to know that, with his profile, it could be that he is being pressed on to a manager for reasons other than football. So, he contacted me directly and asked if I wanted him to come to Milan. I told him,

'Yes.' Only then did we discuss how and when he might play. As it happened, he probably played more than he expected, but the point is that we trusted each other to speak the truth.

My main job in the recruitment process is to say, 'We need this type of player for this position and that type of player for that position.' I might suggest one or two names but the club will draw up a list of players to fit this remit in collaboration with the analytics departments. In the old days it would just be the head coach and the president compiling the list, but football is big business now and many considerations other than simply his performance on the pitch that the player can bring are taken into account, like his age and potential sell-on value, commercial revenues and such things. This is not my job, however. My concern is how they will perform in the team.

Sometimes, when we have a choice between players for the same position, I have an important role to play in choosing the one we should go for. At Real Madrid, when it was between Toni Kroos and another player, I told the general director, 'I know this other player. He drinks a lot and he is not very professional. You have to go for Kroos.' I got Kroos.

It is important to try to recruit people who have the same ideas as you about behaviour and professionalism – people who share your beliefs – and who share the values of the organization they're joining. This is why it is vital for that responsibility and direction to be held by the president and his senior team. Some managers are in the job less than a year, so it cannot be their responsibility to protect the values of the club.

I have never been at a club where I had total responsibility for recruitment. Not even in England, where my general director was often Abramovich himself. I think my friend and former assistant Paul Clement held such a responsibility at Derby County but such full responsibility is too much for any one person. At Manchester United van Gaal was given carte blanche, the same at Everton with Roberto Martínez. But I believe such situations will not last because there's so much relying on this one guy, and he can't do all of these things. For the clubs it doesn't make sense to allow only the manager to dictate recruitment because the manager will, statistically, be there less than two years on average. What then of all the players he has recruited? No, the club must have a policy and the manager must become part of implementing that policy.

When Real Madrid decided to sign a kid from Norway, sixteen-year-old Martin Ødegaard, I thought, 'I don't care if he comes or not, because he's not going to play for me now.' He could go on to be the best player in the world after I'm gone, but I'm not interested in the signing because it isn't of importance to my job. Of course, when he arrived I treated him with the same respect I would give to any young player, but why would I want to be involved in his recruitment? He is being recruited for the future, for other managers after my time.

It is still vital to respect the vision of the owners. Pérez was well known for his *galácticos* approach, where the biggest and most expensive superstars in world football are recruited, so players would arrive and depart who would not necessarily have been my choice, but it was my job to make the team work with whatever assets I was given. It is a waste of time and energy to fight against something that has already happened – you must manage it. After all, that is why we are called managers. If the president decides that, for a PR exercise, he needs the Norwegian boy to play three games with the first team, I will work out a way of doing that. If the president also decides to sell midfielder Xabi Alonso, I must accept that too. Did I want to lose Alonso? No, of course not, but my job was to make it work.

Paris was different. At Real Madrid my eyes were open as to how long my stay would be, but at Paris Saint-Germain I thought I was going to be involved in a long-term project, so I wanted to know more about the academy and the recruitment policies, about everything involved in producing players for the team both at the time and in the future. I was trying to build the culture there and wanted to be fully involved in making sure the players coming in would fit that culture.

Agents play a huge role in recruitment now. Thankfully, this is the domain of the general director, whose job requires him to have relationships with them. I try not to have any dealings with agents, and the clubs I have worked with have rarely asked me to get involved with them. In football the agent can act for both parties, unlike in sports in the US where the agents can act for one party only. So, if the agent is acting for both parties, how can you be sure where his strongest commitment lies? I do not have an agent myself other than my wife, Mariann. I have a very close friend, who advises me when I need it. It probably doesn't hurt that he is one of the best agents in the game.

Maybe my advice should be to marry your agent or, if you're already married, then ask your wife to be your agent. Barcelona right back Dani Alves's wife is his agent. Actually, it's his ex-wife. They'd just broken up and she was negotiating for him when he arrived at Barcelona. She said, 'How can you offer him so little money – he has to feed his wife and children *and* me.' Now, that's an agent playing all the cards at her disposal.

I had a young player at Paris, Adrien Rabiot, who also kept it in the family, but in a different way. He was seventeen years old when I put him in the first-team squad and every day his mother, Véronique, would come to watch training. She really pushed her son and one day she asked to have a meeting with me. We sat down together and Véronique said, 'I am here as a mother and as an agent of my son.'

'Hold on,' I said. 'I'm going to speak with you as his mother, not the agent. The agent has to speak with the president.' That's my rule. Obviously, when the market is open then sometimes the general director or the president will ask me to speak with the agents, but not once the season is under way. It is not the best way.

Onboarding

The job of the manager is to integrate the players who have been recruited into the fabric of the team, which is called 'onboarding' in some circles. It is up to me to communicate to the players what their behaviour should be like outside the club, what is expected of them. Things like eating sensibly, drinking responsibly and living a normal life, by which I mean integrating as quickly as possible into a new culture. This is professionalism and this is what I expect of my players. To return to the issue of culture and language, I can't understand a player who comes to a country and, in two years, is not able to speak the language. Six months should be the maximum. If an old guy like me can do it then so can the players. I think it should be part of their contract, because if it doesn't happen, it usually has a negative effect on his performance. Why would you not want to learn the language? It is unprofessional not to.

Onboarding is handled differently depending on the club. Some clubs have serious infrastructure to handle the process as smoothly as possible. They employ people to help the players find houses, schools – anything the family needs to settle into their new environment. It makes sense for the club to do this: a happy and settled player off the pitch is more likely to be able to concentrate on playing. The players' agents are also usually heavily involved in helping them settle.

As part of the onboarding process, the club usually gives each player help with the language, and every single day he has a relationship with his teammates, in which he can listen, learn and practise. This is key: ultimately, the player has to want to learn.

We would try to buddy the players up. I'd ask Sergio Ramos, who is from Madrid, to look after Kroos or Bale. I would ask this not as an imposition, but just as a suggestion, only if he was willing to. This is the quiet way. In fact, when you have leaders like Ramos, John Terry or Paolo Maldini in the dressing room, they take care of this of their own free will, it is automatic to them, and this is the most effective way of all.

Development

How do you keep developing players such as Ronaldo, who are already at the top? It is easy. These players are so professional that they tell you where they need developing or they are happy to discuss where you think they might improve. These will never be technical improvements, but always to do with game management or analytics or physical information.

With young players it is a little bit different. For the young players you have to do some specific work to improve their limits, to improve their understanding of the game and their role within different systems, and also some technical work in areas where they might be deficient. So, with the eighteen-year-old Ronaldo who signed for Manchester United, it was important that he understood the team dynamics, and within the United system his crossing and decision-making needed work. Sir Alex and his coaches at Manchester would only have been concerned with his technique where it was applied towards the needs of the team. By the time he was at Madrid, it had become a case of working out how we could best get the team to extract the most value from his talent. So, the development needs gradually change as the player grows.

Great players are great decision-makers. They know when to pass, when to shoot, when to defend, when to attack, all for the most benefit to the team. The manager of a very talented player has to convince the player to put this talent to the service of the team – this is how they can continue to develop.

I have to find a way to keep this talent alive and efficient, but to deploy it within the system of the team. I don't want them to sacrifice their unique quality – they have to keep that – and, equally, I have to make the team understand the special value that such players can add. If I didn't have Ronaldo, for example, or I didn't have Zidane, maybe I would play a different system.

While I was at Parma I had the opportunity to buy Roberto Baggio. I always played a 4-4-2 system at the time, so I decided not to sign him because he wanted to play behind the striker, not in a 4-4-2. I realize now that I was wrong to reject him. I didn't want to play him as a forward – I wanted to play him as an offensive midfielder. I refused to change my idea of football because I was not confident, I was unsure. I didn't have the experience, I was a little bit worried, and in the end I knew I'd made a mistake. I should have worked with Baggio and found a way.

I learned my lesson and appreciated the quality to be more flexible with systems when I went to Juventus. I had to change my idea of football to accommodate Zidane, building the system around him rather than forcing him into my preferred 4-4-2. Instead we played three in the back, four midfielders, Zidane in front, plus two strikers. We sacrificed at the back because I didn't want to put Zidane on the left of a 4-4-2 where he was not comfortable. So, Zidane played behind the two front players. He played between the midfield and forwards, between the lines, when we were attacking and he helped – a little – with the midfield when we defended.

With Cristiano Ronaldo I initially thought that the easiest way was to play him with Karim Benzema as a striker. That way, I could play James Rodríguez on the right, with Bale on the left and Modrić and another in the middle. People say that I had to play James because the president spent so much money on him after the World Cup, but for me, this was not a factor. The money does not matter once the player is at the club; I wanted James in the side because of his football qualities. He's unselfish and a hard worker – a true professional.

I was sure Cristiano could play centre forward without a problem and it wouldn't affect his statistics, which he worries about a lot. I spoke with him about this and he said he was not comfortable, that he preferred to play outside, where he can see everything and cut in from a wide starting position. Who am I to argue? I did not want to change his position – how can I change the position of a player who scores sixty goals a season? So, I had to find a solution. I hadn't played a 4-3-3 system very often before, but I had to try it so that Cristiano could play in the position that best suited his talents and, most importantly, from where his talents could be best used for the team.

Andrea Pirlo at Milan was a great example of how a manager can listen to a player, work with him and develop him to add value to the whole squad. I was talking with him about how we had to put a squad together with great quality, because the owner wanted to play attractive football and I had to find someone to fill a deep-lying midfield position. Pirlo simply said to me, 'I can do this.' I was surprised at first, but then I could see the position in my mind and I thought, 'Yes, you could be the right guy after all.'

My worry was that for three years he had played as an attacking midfielder and I didn't know whether he had the condition to change his position. There would be more work and he was not a physically powerful player. He would have to learn to understand how to play this position. I would need to discuss the new defensive responsibilities this role would have, but I didn't want to scare him off straight away after he had come forward with the idea. Instead, I spoke mostly about the attacking demands of the role, how he would be the focal point of the team, our game-changer.

Later, I was able to make him feel comfortable and dispel any doubts about his capacity to do it by explaining that the defensive situation was not so difficult. 'I only need you to be in the right position,' I said. 'You don't have to press, you don't have to tackle, but you must track and be goal-side when it is necessary.' I tried to take away any concerns he might have because I was sure that he could do the job. He didn't have to be Claudio Gentile, after all.

I explained to him his importance in being able to organize the play of the team, how playing deeper would allow him to have more space compared to other attacking midfielders. I tried to fill him with confidence, telling him he was the best one to play this position. Of course, if he had not been convinced about trying it, we wouldn't have done it. Luckily, for me and for Milan and the national side – but not for England – he was excited to give it a go because he didn't have a lot of space in his attacking role and he hadn't played a lot in the last three years as an attacking midfielder – we had a lot of players in these positions. Pirlo was smart and recognized a potential new career path for himself, becoming one of the best deep-lying playmakers in world football and using his talents in the right role for the team.

For me, the solution is never to sacrifice talent by

diminishing it, but always to enable it to flourish, because this is always the best for the team. So, the balance must be not lowering the talent to fit the team, but rather raising the team to fit the talent.

Succession

In business, one of the things that great leaders try to do well is managing the exit of underperforming or redundant staff, handling it with care and sympathy. This is not always true in football, where the ruthlessness of management is often the focus of considerable criticism, but it should be, because it makes good business sense. You never know when you are likely to meet players again in your career. I am very conscious of this.

There haven't been many occasions when it has been necessary for me to discuss a player's exit from the club. One occasion was near the end of my time at Madrid, when Javier 'Chicharito' Hernández came to me to ask about his future. With him it was clear, so I told him, 'I don't know what my own situation is for the future, so I cannot give you an answer. If I stay, I want you to stay also, but that is not my decision.' It is usually the decision of the president and the general director at the big clubs, and this will increasingly be the case as football becomes more corporate.

I have some influence in this, of course. If I decide that a player is not in the team then that fact alone speaks to the general director and he will be thinking of the player as a liability, not an asset. That is when the president will be asking questions. Often, there are more reasons for why a player must leave than just his performance on the field.

So, whether a player leaves the club is not mainly my decision, but the amount of playing time they get is, of course, very much my decision, even if sometimes the president might want it not to be so. Dropping people from the team and putting them on the bench or, even worse, in the stands, and replacing them with another player can be a very delicate thing to manage sometimes. I try to keep players I've dropped motivated by continually communicating with them and keeping an eye on them during training, but still, it can be tricky. The situation with Real Madrid's legendary goalkeeper Iker Casillas was certainly a little bit difficult.

When I arrived at Madrid, Casillas had not been playing under Mourinho, who had preferred to play Diego López. For me, it was a difficult choice because Casillas had such a big history with the club. In such a situation it is always best to fall back on the technical side: If you think that one is better than the other, you put that one in the team. I decided to make Diego López the first-choice goalkeeper and before the first game I told Casillas. I explained to him that, in my opinion, at that moment, Diego López was more ready than he was. He could not dispute this because López had had a full preseason, while Casillas had not.

Maybe there are ten technical aspects for a goalkeeper and nine are equal, but on this particular aspect, Diego

López was just a little bit better. Or, because we are to play a high defensive line, this goalkeeper might be quicker than this one, and that would be the deciding factor. There was not a huge difference between the players, but it was my view that López was more ready than Casillas.

Having made that decision, I didn't then want to keep Casillas eternally second, because I knew that he was an important player for the club. In the end I decided to alternate them, with one playing in the league and the other in the cup competitions.

The conversations with them were hard but fair. Before the start of the Champions League I thought about this for a long time and I decided to play Casillas in the competition. I spoke with Diego López before informing Casillas, telling him that it was important to keep a positive atmosphere in the squad. Once he had been told, only then did I speak with Casillas, telling him that I wanted to give him an opportunity to play. 'I know you are a great goalkeeper,' I said, 'so I don't think it's correct for you to always have to be second-choice.' He said, 'I'm not happy, but I understand your decision. I'll keep working.' There are some conversations that are painful. Despite playing in the cup competitions he was still unhappy. He wanted to be number one in all competitions.

In the end it meant both players were highly motivated. Both Casillas and López could legitimately say that they played in the most important games – López in La Liga and Casillas in the Champions League and Copa del Rey. Over the course of the season, Diego López played thirty-seven games and Casillas played twenty-four. López was genuinely humble, a serious player. He was OK about the Champions League, perhaps because he had a lot of pressure on him with Casillas hovering as number two. It was not so easy for him to be replacing a Madrid legend and so maybe my decision helped to take away some of the pressure from him.

Succession – removing or demoting players or staff, on either a temporary or permanent basis – is difficult, and requires the delicate use of influencing skills and diplomacy to accomplish satisfactorily. Naturally, there will be fallout, but it is essential to remember that one day you might cross the path of that particular person as a boss, a peer or even as a subordinate, and you will be sure to reap what you have sown.

TALENT: THE QUIET WAY

- Speak to your talent (players, workers) firstly and most importantly as *people*.
- Recruit to your values and for cultural fit. Always have in your mind your 'future team' as you go through the building process.
- Try to avoid intermediaries (like agents or even certain board members). The more layers, the more complexity, the more room for misunderstanding. Talk directly to the talent if possible. Your personal relationship with them is the best insurance policy you can have during moments of trauma.
- Coaching great talent is about fine-tuning, not major changes. The level of development needed by those who arrive at the biggest corporations should not be technical, but about managing the game or the business.
- You can't control the talent. You can only provide the right information for them to achieve what they want to achieve; then it is up to them.

- Never forget that the talent will protect itself as its first priority. Talent chooses businesses as much as they are chosen by them.
- Recruit to your budget. This might mean that you have to give younger workers the chance. Don't be afraid to do this; it should be seen as an opportunity.
- When you first engage with the people or talent you will work with forget about the 'X and Os' of how to do the job. Take time to understand them as people; what makes them who they are; who influences their life; who has shaped who they are. The 'How do we drive this bus?' comes after 'Who made the driver of the bus?'.
- For the selfish talent help them to understand the satisfaction and reward that comes with serving the needs of others.
- Take the onboarding of talent seriously. The stronger your culture the harder it is for anyone to join and integrate. Be open, listen and show that you care about them and their family as people. It's the start of the process of gaining 'discretional effort' from them.

- Your job is not to motivate the talent – they should find this within themselves – your job is not to demotivate them.

IN THEIR OWN WORDS . . . THE PLAYERS

DAVID BECKHAM ON CARLO

The first time I had any real interaction with Carlo was when he brought me in on loan at AC Milan. I'd spoken to Adriano Galliani at a more official level, but I'd also spoken to Carlo because I've always thought it's important for a player to speak to the manager himself, just to make sure that he's actually wanted at the club and in the team.

The idea of going to Milan was first mooted by Fabio Capello, who was England manager at the time. I was playing for LA Galaxy and I was talking to him about my chances of being involved with the national side for the World Cup. He said to me, 'You need to go on loan to be involved. You need the right level of football.' When I asked his advice about where I should go, he said, 'You should go to Milan. Carlo will look after you.' That tells you everything you need to know about Carlo.

My first meeting with Carlo was actually in Dubai, where the team were on their Christmas break. Obviously, I knew he was an amazing coach, but I wasn't prepared for what a great guy he was as well. I think he's a manager that any player would love playing under. He commands respect because he's been so successful over so many years, but it's not only that. He's a nice guy and players just want to play and win for him – and I think that's what Carlo has always been about. Don't forget that not only is he a great manager, but he was a great player as well, with the trophies to show for it, and that doesn't happen very often.

When we talk about Carlo being a nice person you also have to understand that on the pitch he is very demanding. He always works the players hard because he knows what it takes to be successful.

When I first arrived in Dubai to join up with the team, I knew that I was never going to be in the starting eleven because there were players who had been there for years and I was only there on loan. I hadn't even thought about it, really. I worked hard and performed well in training and then, in the first game back after the Christmas period, against Roma, I was in the team. Obviously I was pleased, and my relationship with Carlo at that time was great. As a player, the worst thing is when the manager doesn't recognize that you're working hard, but Carlo had seen my efforts. From that moment I knew I would always be happy to play for this man.

When it came to the end of my career in America and I had

the opportunity to go to Paris Saint-Germain for six months it was not a difficult decision. The challenge of being able to help the team win their first trophy in nineteen years, the fact that it was Carlo asking and, of course, that Ibra was there as well meant there weren't many reasons to say no.

In the dressing room his approach is calm. He believes that players should be able to motivate themselves. Some managers shout and get angry as a way of showing authority, whereas Carlo has that authority just because you respect him so much. That calmness he inspires throughout the dressing room helps the players to be calm around him and want to play for him and that is one of his great strengths.

There's not one thing that you could surprise Carlo with on the tactical side of things. Firstly, because he's Italian, and they take this part of the game very seriously there, and secondly, because he knows everything about the game that needs to be known. At Milan, we had constant video sessions and meetings about the other team and the individual players. He surrounds himself with great people and never leaves any stone unturned. That's the type of manager he is and that's why he's had the success he's had and will continue to be successful. He keeps doing things until they're right.

Another important thing about Carlo was that, when the team

was going through a difficult time, he made it all about the manager, putting it all on himself. Even if there were things going on around the club that were disturbing, he would never let it affect the players. He would take all the pressure off us and blame himself – that's what great managers do.

Carlo was very relaxed, but if you weren't playing well, and if you weren't doing the right things or what he'd said to do, then you would know about it. I suppose if there's one thing that gets him angry it's bad attitude – not being 'serious', as he says. Luckily for me, I'd been brought up by another manager who believes it's all about attitude. Carlo says it's about having the right impression of the game and your opponents as well. If you're beating your opponents 3–0 or 4–0 and you're showboating, then that's something Carlo wouldn't like. He's a typical Italian, all about doing things in the right way.

He definitely likes players to be 'serious' at the right times. I was lucky again that I was at a club like Manchester United, where if you were late by a minute then you got fined. Carlo has the same mentality. For him, you have to do things right to be successful and to be the best at the highest level in the game. You have to be professional; you can't just drift through training while not working hard.

Take Ibra, who has played under Carlo for a number of years.

Everyone knows Ibra is one of the greatest footballers in the game, but he's also one of the hardest workers. He gets respect in training because it doesn't matter to him whether he's playing in a World Cup or a five-a-side game, he wants to win – and Carlo is exactly the same. Carlo will accept a certain amount of joking around, and as long as you're doing things in a professional way, then he will be fine with that, but I think he shows his frustration. His team might be winning, but he won't always be happy if the attitude isn't right, and he looks for professionalism even in players stretching and warming up.

Of course, he can lose it, like all of us, I suppose. But it never seems to affect the way the players feel about him. I think the only time I saw him lose it was in the last game of the season when I was at Milan and we were going for a Champions League place. We were winning the game but playing like crap. I couldn't tell you what he was angry about because when he does lose it, he says it in Italian. It's great and unexpected to watch, but it's kind of scary. Thankfully, I'm not fluent in Italian.

I've been lucky to play for great club managers and I couldn't rank them – they all had different styles. But there's one thing they all have in common: they're winners. Every manager has their own way of managing a team and individual players. Sir Alex Ferguson commanded respect and Carlo automatically gets it because he knows everything about the game. He treats the players with great respect, *but only if he gets that respect in return.*

I clearly remember Carlo's last game at AC Milan. I saw in the changing room just how much love the players had for him – and that's not too strong a word. They didn't just love him as a manager, they loved him as a person. To those players, his leaving was like losing a father. Carlo gave a speech in the changing room and he was emotional, but even more emotional were the players who had been with him for years. I'd only played under Carlo for six months at that time and he was talking in Italian and I could only understand part of it, but even I was moved.

Players like Paolo Maldini, Gennaro Gattuso, Filippo Inzaghi and Alessandro Nesta were in tears because they knew that the club was going to change, all because this one man – this one man who has brought so much success to AC Milan – was leaving. As Ibra said later, at PSG, 'Now he's gone you'll recognize how good he was.' Unfortunately, that happens a lot. It's often only when a great manager like him leaves a club that everyone realizes just how influential he was when he was there.

5. The Workplace

There is a great deal of mystique surrounding the inner sanctum of the dressing room, but it has the same dynamics as any workplace. An awareness of the sensitivities of specific environments is an essential part of any leader's toolbox and acclimatizing quickly to these intense environments is something that I have had to do throughout my managerial career.

On the first day at a club, the players and staff show me respect for what I have achieved, as a player and as a manager. After that, they are looking, watching you every day: *What you are doing? How easy is your behaviour? Are you serious, are you professional?* These are the questions going through the players' minds, and it is like sitting an exam every day. If they don't think you can add value to them, the players don't care who you've played for, who you've managed. It works the other way too. If they think you can add value, they don't care whether you've played or not.

It's all about what you can do for them, because talented people are very selfish. They want their talent to be nurtured. To the players, it's all about helping them get better, and if I can't then I'm no use to them.

Dressing Room Leaders

When I arrived at Chelsea I thought that settling into a new environment, away from the comfort of my home country, would be my biggest challenge. Admittedly, all the organization was in place to help me assimilate, but would the dressing room present a different challenge? Although there were many foreign players at the club, there was also a very strong English presence there who formed the core of the club and would need to be on board if I was to be a success. As it turned out, this actually made my job easier than it might have been. I found excellent English players there – John Terry, Frank Lampard, Ashley Cole. They were professional in training and on the pitch, with the right attitude and great intensity, and this all made for a pleasant surprise. When you add in players like Petr Cech, Didier Drogba and Michael Ballack, you have a central group of clear leaders – different styles of leadership, but all strong characters – and a great example for the others.

I set about creating relationships with each of these players separately. I like to speak with players not only about tactics, but also about personal things, and to joke around. Everything should not *always* be so serious at work. The personal interest is important to me for its own sake, in that I am interested in and care about each individual player, and it also helps to build the relationship for when the hard decisions have to come later in the season. It's important to do this early in a job. With some people it is easier to build this bond, while with others it can be more difficult. Drogba was not so easy at the beginning because he was a little wary and didn't have a lot of confidence in me.

It is always important to have great leaders in the team. They do not need to be like me; instead, they need to complement me and be respected by the rest of the team. Ideally, there should be more than one leader. At Chelsea, there were a rare number of leaders in the dressing room and at Madrid there were the likes of Ramos, Ronaldo and Pepe.

Leaders can only lead if followers believe in them. It doesn't matter why they believe in them. It could be their personality, like Ibrahimović or John Terry, or it could be their example, like with Franco Baresi, whom I played with at Milan, or Ronaldo. It can be both. This is how I like to think of the leaders, as either personality leaders or technical leaders. A personality leader uses his strength of character to lead. He is always a talker in the team, speaking to his teammates a lot, often shouting across the pitch, helping everyone out. He should be positive and fearless and he will always step forward when the occasion demands it.

A technical leader will not speak as much, but lead by example. Such players are always very professional, someone for all the youngsters to aspire to be like. The technical leader is the player who has the most knowledge on the pitch. They train hard and play hard and behave correctly off the pitch too, in the spirit of the culture of the club. I've found it is effective to have a combination of these types of leader, while being aware that the qualities are not mutually exclusive – a player can be a strong personality and set a great example. There might also be what I call a political leader – a player who is seen as a leader by the press and the fans as a figurehead for the club, but these leaders are rarely viewed as such by their teammates.

Sometimes players of Ronaldo's stature are not interested in the rest of the team, just themselves, but this is not true of Cristiano. He is a technical leader – so serious, so professional in everything he does.

At Milan I was lucky to have Paolo Maldini, a personality leader *and* a technical leader, an idol for the club, who, like Ramos at Madrid, was a strong character, never scared, never worried, always positive and talked to his teammates a lot. There was Andrea Pirlo, who was a bit of a loner, a little bit timid, but such an example in his play – a technical leader. Alessandro Nesta was also a good example – a different style to Maldini – and Gennaro Gattuso, another. Andriy Shevchenko was both a strong personality and strong technically, but he was very focused on his own game. He was a striker – what can you do? It was the same with Hernán Crespo, great for the team simply because he was so driven to score.

Of course, where there are so many strong people there are always going to be clashes, and these must be dealt with quickly. One time at Chelsea there was a fight between Michael Ballack and Joe Cole after Ballack was really strong in the tackle with Cole during training. He made contact

and Joe reacted – they started to front up. In football sometimes you make contact, the other guy gets angry and reacts
and the whole thing escalates over silly things. When there
is a fight it is usually because one or both players are a little
bit hot and overreact – it's rarely a big deal.

Before I intervene in such matters, I wait to see if they
will work it out between themselves. If that doesn't happen
then I send them to the dressing room. Sometimes, if it's
really bad, I will follow them into the dressing room after a
short while to make sure they haven't taken things too far,
but usually by the time I get there it is already solved and I
walk away. If not, I will speak with them together and then
individually, and maybe the day after, when the argument
has been settled, I will reinforce this with the group: 'Yes-
terday there was a fight. Let's not let it happen again because
we are teammates and we need to be together if we're going
to achieve anything.' With Cole and Ballack, I spoke with
them together, they shook hands and it was done.

Maybe I have been lucky in that I have never had
long-running feuds like the one I was told about between
Andy Cole and Teddy Sheringham at Manchester United,
but Sir Alex dealt with that in his way and the team's success wasn't affected. There are always going to be players in
the dressing room who have closer relationships with some
than others, but they all must understand that they cannot
let bad relationships affect the game. That is in nobody's
interest. It applies to me, too. I don't have the same personal relationship with all the players – with some I am

more comfortable than others – but in the dressing room all are the same. They must know that I treat them all the same because I am a professional. Any hint of favouritism can be deadly.

The Captaincy

Sometimes too much is made of the captaincy in football, but it can be important. Some players want to be captain and grow even more if you give it to them. Others don't want, or need, to be captain – they are natural leaders. When I offered Ibrahimović the captaincy at Paris Saint-Germain, he refused it, saying he was not sure how long he would stay at the club so to be captain would be wrong. But that didn't stop him being a natural leader through his personality.

In my own playing career, I was only ever captain for a short time, at Roma. It was a little bit strange because, to be honest, I didn't want to be captain. Sven-Göran Eriksson was the manager and the captain was midfielder Agostino Di Bartolomei. When Di Bartolomei was sold to Milan, it was usually the way that the most senior player would become the captain. This was Bruno Conti, a World Cup winner. He also didn't want the role, and there were still other players in front of me – I was only twenty-five, twenty-six years old – but Eriksson decided that I would be his captain. He asked the other senior players if it was a good idea to appoint me and everyone said, 'OK.'

I was a little bit surprised to get it, but it was an honour. As things turned out, it was to be for only one year. I went to Milan, where Franco Baresi was the captain. He wasn't about to step aside for anyone, let alone a newcomer. Baresi was a technical leader. He didn't speak a lot, but he was really serious – and very strong. His strength came from the example he set, with his values as a professional and his work ethic. Maldini learned a lot from Baresi.

In my short time as captain I never encountered any real problems, but that is because the figure of the captain was not as important then as it is now – in those days it was more of an honour than a job. Now, the captain is more involved, speaking with the manager and referees and playing a more important role in the squad, as a reference for the players and the owners. Because squads are bigger now there is more responsibility on the captain to set an example to the players who are promoted from the academy.

Sometimes, as a manager, when you arrive at a new club you find a captain already in place, like John Terry was at Chelsea, and that takes care of itself. Sometimes, however, like it was at Paris Saint-Germain, you have to change the captain. When I arrived in Paris the captain was Mamadou Sakho, who was only twenty-one years old. I kept him in place until I could get a more suitable player in, and when Thiago Silva arrived he was made captain. I took this decision not because Sakho was not good in the role – he had a lot of qualities – but because there was a lot of pressure on him. He was from Paris, bred from the academy and very young, so by taking the responsibility away from him I took away a little bit of pressure. Thiago didn't speak a lot but, like Baresi, he was a role model for the other players.

Although as manager I must have a particularly close relationship with the captain, it has to be a professional relationship, not a personal one. There has to be some distance between me and all the players, even the captain. I learned this from Maldini at Milan. He helped me a lot when we were teammates and I thought that it would be the same when I was the boss, but Maldini changed his behaviour more than me when I became his manager. I still looked at him as if he were my teammate, but he treated me as 'the boss'. I could not have made that change so easily, but when Maldini made it clear that we must have a new, professional relationship I understood why. I was grateful to him.

It is not always the captain who is the main leader. At Madrid, Ramos was not the team's captain – that honour belonged to Casillas – but Ramos was the leader, especially because Casillas was not playing all the games. Casillas was the captain because he had been brought through the academy and had played a lot of matches for the club, but Ramos was the strongest leader.

In Madrid it's a strange setup. The club has one captain and three vice-captains, and it is this group who speak with the president as representatives of the players about such things as bonuses. In my time the captain was Casillas and the vice-captains were Ramos, Marcelo and Pepe. They were the senior players, the ones with the most time at the club. If you see the team pictures, you will see the president in the centre; above the president there is the manager; then, flanking the president you will see Casillas, Ramos, Pepe, Marcelo.

So, at Madrid it was a fluid setup. You had the captain, but there were other leaders, Ramos chief among them, while at Chelsea the main leader, John Terry, was also the captain. The benefit of having a strong and secure captain is that other players have the opportunity to lead in their own way.

Players like Terry, Maldini and Ramos show personality in every moment – when they speak before the game, when they speak with their teammates, when they speak on the pitch, in their attitude in training. The captain is important, but having leadership throughout the team is critical. If you can get the balance right and have both, then you have the best chance to win.

Dressing Room Rules

The dressing room today is the same dressing room as when I was playing, twenty, thirty years ago. The relationship between the players hasn't changed. What has changed is what goes on outside the dressing room. Players now have to deal with commercial pressures from sponsors, agents and a range of other external sources. These pressures also come from within the club, but *outside* the dressing room. Inside, it is the same as it has always been.

Of course, in the top division you have the cream of the talent – the superstars. As I have said throughout this book, it's very important to communicate with this talent, to have a professional relationship – and for them to have this relationship with their teammates. The superstar player must know that, while his salary might be many times that of other players in his own team, he cannot expect privileges. He is subject to the same rules as everyone – it really is a team game. This is and always has been a law of the dressing room.

Players have to understand that we need flexibility and equality for the good of the group, and it is my job to convince them to abide by this principle. The problem is that players often feel that they know what is best for them – or they believe their agent when he tells them how special they are.

These laws of the dressing room are encoded in the same way as any workplace – people know what is acceptable and unacceptable behaviour. It all harks back to culture. The difference between culture and climate is that we want the former to be permanent but we know that the latter can be changeable. It is the same with implicit and explicit rules of the workplace. Explicit rules are changeable, but implicit rules represent the underlying, accepted culture.

Implicit rules are difficult to manage because they go to the heart of what you always hope to be the unspoken code

of the players and the club. I only have one implicit rule
and that is to be professional, but I cannot always control
this because I can only control what happens on the pitch
and at the training ground. I can control the professionalism of the players when I am with them, but I cannot hope
to control them when they are at home or away from the
club. It is for this reason that the communication within
the relationship is so important. You have to communicate
what is expected of the players at all times, even when
they're away from the team, not only with words but also by
showing them. I can tell the players that they have to be
professional – eat properly, sleep properly – but I cannot
force them. I can't monitor them every day, so I have to
convince them through influencing and through trusting
them. I do this by referencing those players who are the
best professionals.

At Real Madrid, there was a problem in training one day
when one of the players suddenly left the pitch and returned
to the dressing room without my permission. I went to see
him afterwards. I said to him, 'You have to train. You don't
want to be known for this kind of reaction.' He complained
that another player wasn't working hard enough in the session, that he was cheating his teammates.

I said, 'But today there were sixteen players out there and
you focused on one player that didn't train properly. The
other fourteen players trained well. Why do you have to
speak to me about the player who doesn't run, doesn't
work – why do you pick that one player? Why don't you

watch the players who are world-class professionals on the pitch? Don't be focused on the one player who has bad behaviour today, because this is just an excuse for you. You think that because there is one player who doesn't work properly, you can do the same. This is not what great players do.

'If your teammates looked at you on some days and did the same thing as you then we'd never finish a training session with all the team on the pitch, because there are times when you don't train properly yourself. So then I would have to find an excuse for you.'

I told him that I had explained it to the other player as well, telling him that if he wanted to be valued like Ronaldo, he too must score sixty goals a season for many years. 'Ronaldo is who you must reference,' I said to the complaining player. 'You have to change your attitude; you have to be focused on the players who trained well.'

He said, 'Now I understand.'

It was the same with Florent Malouda. At Chelsea we used to use GPS devices to collect data about each player's performance, and in the middle of the first training session, Malouda removed the GPS device and went to the dressing room. I followed him and asked him why he had left.

'Because I'm tired of this GPS crap,' he said. 'It is just to control me and I don't like to be controlled. I don't want to train with this.' I told him, 'You have to train with this. It's not to control you – it's to control my job.' I tried to explain the situation and I told him, very quietly, that his behaviour was not acceptable. 'If you don't go outside,' I added, as Vito Corleone himself might have said, 'I have to kill you.' He went outside.

After that we managed the GPS issue better. The players really didn't like using it every day and, in my view, it's not always so important to use it – so we compromised. GPS is essential only when you have a strong session, to stop you damaging the players, so I said, 'Let's use it for four days out of six.' Then the problem was that some of the players, particularly the British players, wanted to use the GPS *every* day. They couldn't understand that, to me, if you use GPS for four days it is the same result – nothing changes. 'Why can't we work harder?' they'd ask. This is the British way.

I am reminded of what Paul Clement told me about the World Cup-winning English rugby coach Clive Woodward. He said that there are two kinds of people – energizers and energy sappers. When you see the behaviour of a player on the training pitch like that I've just described at Real Madrid, you can see clearly an energy sapper. Their behaviour takes away your energy. It can take away the energy of the whole group. It certainly took away the energy of the player who left the pitch.

It is the energizers who are the reference points for everybody, including me. Players such as Sergio Ramos, he gives you energy – when he speaks, when he trains. Cristiano, Pepe, Benzema – these are all 'energizers'. When I say to a player, 'You have to be professional,' they must understand that I'm saying this for their benefit. I don't want to spell out this law, which I believe should be implicit, so by referencing the other players, I can *show* it. They can see it with their own eyes and understand how to behave.

If somebody arrives at the club who does not behave professionally, I have to try to manage them by being totally professional myself on the training ground. I cannot allow my feelings about the player's behaviour to allow me to unduly affect my work with him. However, this is difficult. During my career the manager was always a big example; first I had my father and after that I had a manager. An extension of the family. Now, for the players, the manager is not as important a reference. He is still an example, but not like before. Now they have their own football family, their own frame of reference: their agent; the press. The manager is not as important now as he was, so the personal relationship is not so easy to establish. But day by day, you have to build a stricter relationship with the player as they begin to understand the implicit rule – to meet the standards of professionalism demanded by me and the club.

There are other implicit rules unique to different dressing rooms around the world. In Milan, I was used to training at three in the afternoon, but at Chelsea the players were used to training at eleven in the morning. You cannot start training at three in the afternoon in London, because in winter it's dark before you finish at five. (Also, if you train in the afternoon it means you can't get down to the betting shop afterwards for the start of the racing.) These implicit rules are an accepted part of the culture.

Of course, I could make new, explicit rules. I have that power, in theory. I could tell the players, 'We now train at seven in the morning,' but this is not the right way. This is just to show power. It is always best to use soft power, *quiet* power with the players, to influence and have them follow the implicit rules because they *believe* in them.

There are times when it is important to use both implicit and explicit rules. I hope all the players who play for me know my non-negotiables and my most important rule is to train properly – always give 100 per cent in training. You need to know this if you want to play for me. I cannot allow you just to learn from the others – this takes too long. I have to tell you, then the others will constantly reinforce. They will explain when you are crossing the line. 'The boss won't like that,' they'll say.

It is essential that any non-negotiables are both explicitly stated and implicitly reinforced by players' behaviour on the training ground. If I can point to another player's behaviour as an example it's much easier than having to describe it.

There will always come a time when a player wants to test you, and then you are forced to weigh your principles against expediency. In my first year at Chelsea, with seven games to go, we had a meeting before our game with Aston Villa. Didier Drogba arrived thirty minutes late, so for this reason he didn't play. Not because I was upset, but because he needed to be present at the meeting. I had presented the tactical plan for the game, explaining it all to the players, and I couldn't allow Drogba special consideration. Nobody was allowed to miss this meeting.

Without him in the team we won, 7–1. His replacement, Nicolas Anelka, didn't score, but he played a fantastic game. He killed Aston Villa with movement. The game after, we played Manchester United at Old Trafford and again Drogba didn't play, this time not because he was late, but because Anelka had played so brilliantly against Aston Villa. This is the law of the dressing room – everyone the same, no special privileges. Everyone must be professional. I brought Drogba on as a substitute in the match and he scored our second – and what would become decisive – goal. There were no hard feelings between us as he produced the perfect response to being dropped from the team.

Sometimes these incidents go beyond being mere testing and become unacceptable. The players must know where the line is, as you cannot expect people to accept the rules if they don't know what they are. You must communicate these early in the relationship. There are a lot of things that cannot be tolerated – continually arriving late to training is one and being disrespectful of teammates another. If you're disrespectful to my staff, then that's it. That's unacceptable.

These non-negotiables are about behaviour, and only behaviour. They are not about mistakes on the pitch. If this behaviour is towards me, then I can respond and deal with it, but players who think they can disrespect my staff because they are not the boss – no. This is not right. I have to defend their status. This kind of thing affects the character of the team, who we *are* as a team, and it is not up for negotiation with me. Players know that I am the ultimate decision-maker but they need to respect the team who are assisting me. They should know that any attack on my management team is an attack on me.

I had a problem with one particular player for this reason. He was disrespectful to my assistant, Paul Clement, during a training session and I sent him straight to the dressing room. When I spoke with him afterwards I told him, 'It's unacceptable. I will be telling the president that I want you to go.' And he went, eventually, but from that moment on, the trust was gone.

THE WORKPLACE: THE QUIET WAY

- Your responsibility as a leader is to those you lead.
- Influence beats coercion.
- Kill feuds as quickly as possible. Top talent can be very fragile, sustained conflict can seriously change the energy of the group.
- Encourage the staff to take ownership for the environment and the culture of the workplace. The workplace is their second home, where they spend a lot of time. Let people put their own stamp on it.
- Encourage the energizers, remove the energy sappers.

IN THEIR OWN WORDS . . . THE PLAYERS

JOHN TERRY ON CARLO

When Carlo was appointed Chelsea manager, I'd heard really good things about him – his man-management top among them – so I was curious to meet him. He'd worked with some of the best players in the world, players that I'd looked up to during my career, and yet I was still surprised at how good he actually was. His man-management was the best I've ever had in any of my managers, but what really impressed me were his training sessions, his understanding of players and people, which I don't think a lot of managers nowadays get. He treats people as human beings, whether you win, lose or draw.

You know his training is excellent because he's coached the best teams in the world, which speaks for itself, but it's the personal touches – asking about the family, caring about the off-field stuff – the little things. This, for me, is why the players love him. Instead of being distant, it was always that group mentality.

I've seen him go off on one after games – not often, but I've seen it. He doesn't accept losing easily. He would have these occasional rants, where no one says anything and you listen and take it on board, and then the next minute he's your best mate again. He'd be coming down the back of the bus after a defeat saying, 'We'll be all right. We go again in three days – we'll win, no worry.' The little touches.

He's coached Paolo Maldini, Alessandro Costacurta, Alessandro Nesta, these absolutely top central defenders. I liked to pick his brains on, for example, what they did after training or what they did to improve their game. I was desperate to know about that process. How did he work with those players in my position who were probably some of the best ever? What were those conversations like? Were they one-to-one conversations, with the back four only, or within the team?

With me it was predominantly one-to-one. Whether he meant it or not, he said, 'JT, you're up there with them – you just keep doing what you're doing.' It made me feel like one of them, one of these guys I've looked up to my whole career. In fact, I don't really care if he meant it or not because he made me feel like a million dollars when he was at Chelsea.

Listen, I've played in big games, and in all of those he brought out the best not only of me but also of the other players. He would make us feel ten feet tall in the press, at just the right time. He kept everyone together, which I'd not seen in a long time, and to keep a group of twenty-five top players happy the whole time isn't easy. Obviously, you've got the eleven in the team, but everybody forgets about the other fourteen players who don't play, who are cheesed off because they're not playing. These are the guys who train on their own the day after the game while the other players are warming down and getting ready for the next game. The sessions need to be well run, he needs to be there and active in them, and he was; he was there for every session, always visible.

His door was always open to everybody, and nowadays I don't think you get that too often. I think that you get managers closing their doors and thinking solely about the first team, but he was interested in the academy boys. He knew everyone's names, the young kids included, and I know that, as a player who came through here myself, it meant the world to the younger kids that Ancelotti knew their names.

Carlo was smart when he first arrived. He recognized that we had been through a period under Mourinho with a lot of success, and that many of those players were still here. So, Carlo wasn't one of those managers who comes in and says, 'Right, this is my way. This is the only way I think and it's going to be my way or no way at all.' No, he came in and spoke with the more experienced players as a group and as individuals and said, 'Listen, obviously I've got my ideas, but you guys have known great things for the last few years here. You need to give me a bit of insight into what you think worked really well and why you think you were so successful. Also, how you want things, how you enjoy things.'

I'm not saying he agreed with everything, but to be prepared to take on board the likes of myself, Lamps, Didier and Petr Cech – the spine of the team – was a great start to our relationship. It remained that way. It wasn't for show; he genuinely wanted our input. He wanted to know what kind of daily routine we were used to, what we felt made the players tick.

Of course, he had his own ideas. He certainly brought on the tactical side of things. At Milan, he had liked to do the tactics a couple of days before the game. For me, that never worked in our environment in England and when we said this to him, he took that on board. He would then mix it up, doing the tactics the day before a game, a bit of team shape and, depending on the game, would either name the team the day before or on the day of the game, especially if it was an evening kick-off. The point is that he had actually listened and, again, I don't see many managers now coming in and listening like Carlo did. Some are still all about it being either their way or no way. Once you know someone is listening, you become more comfortable coming up with your own ideas.

He had to change the way he had been used to training. In Italy they clearly separate the physical from the tactical when they train and integrating it, as we do here, was new to him. You could see him really thinking about it. You get this idea of him being quite scholarly, thinking about the game: 'Hang on – this might just work.'

He was open to ideas. We had a team of nutritionists and analysts, so we always used to wear heart-rate monitors, GPS and the like during games, and they wanted to bring that information into training. Because he'd come from the mentality of 'save it all for the weekend', he was shocked by the likes of me, Lamps and Ash kind of charging into tackles. You could see him thinking, 'No, no, no – we don't do that,' but he never actually said it. Instead he'd say, 'That's your way so you continue to do it because it's working for you and has obviously worked in the past. Just be careful.'

He'd have one guy standing on the sidelines watching everyone's heart-rate monitor during training, and if they went into the red zone a little too much, he would ask them to pull out or take it a bit easier. Nine times out of ten the player said no, often because it was the English lads and the ones who really grafted putting in a shift, but again he listened and was receptive to everything. He brought a lot of fresh and new ideas, not only to the first team, but also to the club as a whole; the academy still uses them today.

Paul Clement was here with him, whom he was obviously nurturing and trying to develop, so occasionally Clem would take the sessions, but Carlo would take 90 per cent of them. Even if he wasn't taking the session himself, he would be there.

One of the things that he was obsessed about, which was great for me and the other defenders, was working with the back five. We'd work on movement and shape all the time, getting the distance between players right – that sort of stuff. As I said, because of his history, the defensive unit was keen to work with him. Those sessions were intense – short and sharp. Again, this showed how he knew players. We would do the sessions in small patterns of five- or ten-minute blocks, because he understood that you couldn't do them for thirty or forty minutes. Players get bored and want to play five-a-side – we want the ball.

When we worked on shape, one centre back would push the ball and the others would come in and all of a sudden you're doing it instinctively. We were so well drilled going into games, which is why we had such a great period under him. Everyone knew their position, and it wasn't because we were spending three or four hours of the day on tactics; it was his knowledge, his understanding. He'd know it was better to dip your toe in there, come out and have a bit of fun, then get back in there, before you get your head right the day before a game. He'd know when it was time to switch on and get serious, and equally he was happy for it to be a little bit more relaxed during the week. Two days before a match, though, you could see him get into his game zone, and that rubbed off on everyone.

He was aware that Chelsea was a big club and losing was not an option. He would say that in smaller clubs some inconsistency was OK, but not with a big club. We had to have a big-club mentality in his eyes. Mourinho also had that kind of mentality. He didn't accept losing at all, even in training; he couldn't get his head round it. I think because the games in England come thick and fast, Carlo adapted well. You don't get time to dwell on it for a week. The Italian league was a bit different with a whole week between games; here the games come at the weekend, Wednesday, the weekend again, and early kick-offs, late kick-offs, Bank Holidays, Sundays.

At times, things would be going well on the pitch and you'd come in 2–0 up at half-time, thinking, 'We've got this, three points in the bag,' and he'd go off on one. All of a sudden everyone's back on their toes, ready for the second half. When you're a young player you think, 'Why has the manager gone mad there?' But when you're a little bit older, like myself and Lamps, you take a step back and think, 'He's been clever there – we were going to get sloppy.' We'd go back out there and make it 3–0 and then control possession and that's the end of the game.

He knew exactly how to bring the best out of everyone and keep everyone's heads in the game for the second half. As you get older you look back and think, 'That's what separates the best for me – the little things.' I guess it's like any business – at the very top level the differences are so small that it's the little things that make the difference.

This hatred of losing and obsession with winning is something that links the great managers – the attitude that it's not acceptable to lose. You train how you play, and that mentality is carried from the manager down through the squad – it rubs off on everyone. I've seen it first-hand with some of the best and it's not a good place to be when you've lost. It could even be a small-scale game. I remember games in training a couple of days before a match, where it's relaxed and you might be on the losing side, 2–0 or 3–0, and Carlo would come in the dressing room after and quietly tell us that it was not acceptable. 'We don't lose,' he'd say. 'We take the same mentality of the weekend into training.'

Carlo always used to say that your attitude and mentality

doesn't impact only on the first team, but on the reserves too. They will know that the mentality within that group of twenty-five players, not just the starting eleven, is that it's not acceptable to lose, and this creates a legacy. Wherever I go I carry Carlo's mentality with me, and now it is me who is leaving the legacy.

When you come over to the first team, the mentality is that you do not lose, whether it's a five-a-side game in training or a competitive match, and that legacy still remains. You look at Lamps, he has left and eventually I'm going to go, but you'd like to think that the legacy we've all left remains. I'd like to think that, regardless of anything, that's the attitude within the club.

The other thing the great leaders have is a big-game mentality. Carlo, Mourinho – they're both big-game managers. In England, anyone can beat anyone, but when you play those top teams – the Manchester Citys, Liverpools, Arsenals and Manchester Uniteds – you get a sense of how important they are from the manager. Two days before a game we'll touch on it, then the day before we'll touch on it slightly again, with that little bit more detail. We'll talk about their special players. Let's say Rooney, for example. 'He likes to get the ball in between the midfield and defence,' Carlo would say. 'So if you go in tight on him that creates space behind for the centre forward, who likes to go that way, so we let Rooney have it.' He'll walk you through what needs doing, and again it's that little attention to detail. Not thirty or forty minutes, because that's not what players want. Short and sharp conversations, with the group and with you as an individual. 'Tell me, what's your job?' he'll say, and it's all about the detail.

Being able to pick that whole group of players up, to run through brick walls, play through injuries – it's a testament to Carlo. I've seen players play through injuries, taking injections to get them through it, when they shouldn't really have been out there at all, because they wanted to perform for Carlo Ancelotti. In all of my time as a player, I know that, once you strip everything back, it comes down to this: you go that extra mile for people who care about you as a person.

Those special touches, when he asks questions like, 'How's your dad? I heard he's not been well,' they mean a lot. You think, 'Bloody hell, how do you even know that?' He knows because he genuinely cares, and he takes the time to care. That's what makes him the very best. He is, for me, the ultimate.

6. Responsibility

Decision-making

Making decisions is an inevitable part of being a leader in any industry. In order to make progress every day, decisions need to be made about the training, the players, who is in the team, the opposition. Within a game, decisions have to be made quickly and confidently. Shall I make a substitution? Do I need to make a tactical tweak? If they're not made fast, it can be too late. Time is always moving on during a match and there is no room for indecision – it can kill you.

I am convinced that 'getting things done' in a job is integrally linked to the speed and focus with which decisions are made. The clearest example of decision-making in my industry can be seen on the pitch. I am always impressed by the manner in which the top players are differentiated from the rest primarily by their decision-making and its effect upon the team.

Take the true greats – the likes of Maradona, Pelé, Cruyff. If you were to watch a film of them playing and pause it just before they made their pass, you could ask a hundred coaches where they should play the ball and they would all say the same thing: 'It should go there.' When you press play, the film will show the ball going exactly there. Great players invariably play that 'correct' ball – they make the right decision. Naturally, everybody wants to score, but if somebody else is in a better position, they make the right decision to pass. It's these decisions that, over the course of a match, decide who wins and loses.

Players have to make these decisions in an instant; examples from today's game are Ronaldo and Ibrahimović. Players like Ibra will always make the right decision for the team, not only in the game but also in training. Many say that it is nature, not nurture, that gives these players this ability – but we know it can be trained. When I trained Cristiano at Madrid he already had this ability, but if you look at him in his early days at Manchester United you see a different, more selfish player at the start. Sir Alex and his staff trained him to be a team player. That's the difference between an *engaged* player (who is fully committed) and an *aligned* player (whose commitment always works for the greater good of the team). You need them to be both.

My decisions are not made in split-seconds, like the players', though I do have to make quick and important calls during a match. More generally, I have to make strategic, tactical and operational decisions. Strategically, we have to play good football. By 'good football' I do not mean any particular style of play, but rather that we have to be efficient both offensively and defensively. We have to understand the basics of what works when we have the ball and what works when the opposition has the ball. Deciding on one without the other will not succeed over time. Maybe it will work in one game, but not in the long run. This is the difference between league football and cup football, and it is why the challenge for the coach is always to win the league. Of course, for the owner it might be to win the Champions League, as it was at Real Madrid for me, and so the coach has to think in a different way to achieve this goal. This is why winning a treble – domestic cup, league and Champions League – is so difficult. Even when it has been done, I still can't believe that it is possible.

So, strategic decisions should be long term. However, the pressure from the owners and the fans is for today. To that extent the strategic decisions become strongly influenced by the owners. I might, such as when I was involved in what I thought would be a big project and long term at Paris Saint-Germain, want to buy or promote from the academy a certain type of player for the long-term benefit of the team, but I have to listen to the owner, who might want a player from the outside, or a young player to be promoted for commercial reasons. I have to listen to this and accommodate it. My decisions, therefore, tend to become more short term and mostly tactical, about how the team that I have can deliver the goals that the owner wants. When you spend a long time at a club, such as I did at Milan, with the security that brings, you are more able to be involved in implementing strategic decisions, while at the likes of Real

Madrid decisions must by necessity become short-term and tactical. Ultimately, it is the owner who owns the brand and sets out the policy and the strategy. In one way we are lucky in football because we mostly have very clear ownership. I look at companies like Volkswagen and see complex ownership, and maybe that's why it's in so much trouble with the emissions scandal.

Tactically, you have to use the team at your disposal so that all the component parts, the players and the staff, are able to be efficient in the way I have described as good football. The tactical decisions become part of the longer-term strategy in this way. My job is to create a system of play using the characteristics of the players and to make the players as comfortable as possible with that system. I believe that, in general terms, the best system is 4-4-2 because it creates the most balanced team, certainly defensively. It mirrors the shape of the pitch, a rectangle. But, as I've said, the players are the most important. If it is better for Ronaldo not to play as a second forward, OK, let's try 4-3-3. At the end at Real Madrid, we were able to switch, during the game, from 4-4-2 defensively to 4-3-3 offensively.

Operational decisions are the day-to-day choices I must make. For me, the most important of these involve the players, because it is only with the players that you are able to build the system. If I have to explain to a player why I decided to leave him out of the team, then I must handle this properly. If I decide to reduce the training workload after a testing series of fixtures, then I must do this also.

There comes a point with decision-making, particularly in those you make day-to-day, when you need to know where you can adopt a little bit of flexibility and where you have to be strict. You have to decide where, for you personally, it is OK to be flexible. If I decide to have training at midday and the players come to me and say, 'Why don't we train at eleven? It's better for us then, because we have time to go home and have lunch with our family,' what difference does it make to me? However, once we have agreed on a time, then I have to be strict. It's easier when the players make the decisions, the rules, to hold them to these rules. Former England rugby coach Clive Woodward says the same. Get the players to agree to the rules at the outset, but then it is my job to hold them to their own rules. The negotiation and flexibility come in the decision-making, but the strictness is applied once the decision has been made.

One thing that I work on constantly and where I think I have improved with greater experience is my tendency at times to be too patient. Sometimes I can take a little too long to make the decision. I like to think coolly about such things, take in all the angles, but I can certainly overthink the situation. Sometimes I should use less rationality and more instinct. But then again, sometimes it pays to be patient. It is all about getting the right balance.

Early in my managerial career I made myself crazy trying to choose between two centre forwards for a big game. I was awake all night, thinking it through, tossing and turning, and still couldn't decide. In the morning, the first person

I saw at the club was the doctor, and he told me that one of the two centre forwards was sick and couldn't play. I didn't have to make the decision – it was out of my hands. I have, of course, got better at making these decisions with experience and, despite my sleepless night, learned a valuable lesson that day: I try not to announce who will play and who will be on the bench too early, because if you tell one player he's playing and the other he's not, and then something happens to the player you've picked, you have to go back to the first one. He might not have prepared as fully as he should because he thinks he will not play. It's always a balance.

Getting decisions right or wrong seems an easy thing to quantify, but I don't believe it to be so. When the results of my decision prove not to be good, does that mean it was the wrong decision? No. It only means that it turned out to be wrong. When I make a decision I always think that it's the right decision at the time, otherwise why would I take it? I have no regret because, with the information at my disposal, I did what I thought was best. I can't change it. While it is important to look back and analyse where things have gone wrong, it is vital not to dwell unnecessarily on them. This will kill you.

When we were preparing for the Champions League final in 2007 against Liverpool I had to decide between Alberto Gilardino and Filippo Inzaghi for the striker's position. The players and the club made it clear they thought Gilardino was the one, but in ten games of Champions League football he had only scored two goals. Inzaghi, however, had an excellent record in European competition. He had scored many

Champions League goals. So, I took a decision to put Inzaghi in the team and he scored two goals in the final.

To me, this was the right decision, even if he hadn't scored, because it was *my* decision. I am the one who must live with the decision, so I want it to be mine. If I had any regrets, it would be if it wasn't my decision. After all, I get paid to make these kind of decisions, and sacked if I get them wrong.

If you asked me how I came to this decision, even after considering it all rationally, I would have to say that in the end I trusted my instinct, despite what everyone around me was saying. Sometimes you make a decision and there's not always a logical reason for it. It's just a gut feeling. It's not always easy to explain to the players either.

If I have to choose between Ronaldo and a player fresh from the academy to play on the left for Real Madrid, the decision is easy, and it's also easy to explain to the player from the academy why he does not play. However, if I have to choose between James Rodríguez and Ángel Di María, it is not so easy. I cannot say one player is better than the other, and even if I thought this, I cannot say this to them. It will likely come down to instinct. If it's just my feeling on the day, then I have to do my best to explain that it's what is best for the team. The player left out won't be happy, of course, but he will accept it. Players are never happy if they're not playing.

I see myself as a pragmatist when it comes to making decisions. I have to accept that I must be willing to accommodate the strategies, policies and even the whims of the owners. I hope that I have been able to do this and remain true to my own ideals. Managing the conflicting ideas and egos of talented players and owners is one of the core attributes of a quiet leader. It is my guiding notion that it is simply rational to concentrate only on those things you can affect. Those that are out of your control must be rejected for consideration.

Naturally, I have my own views on the strategic, tactical and operational decisions at the team level, and I must also acknowledge that I will rarely be involved in the strategic decisions concerning the organization. All such team decisions are, for me, intimately related to maintaining the relationships with the players, which is central to quiet leadership.

Anger and Setbacks

Anger is a natural reaction when things don't go as we want, or when players don't behave or perform as we would like. A leader must be careful about exhibiting anger. While it can be a useful tool for some, for many it can result in a loss of control and professionalism, which will always be counter-productive. I am not someone who is angered easily. I find that remaining calm helps me understand and analyse a situation. Anger is instinctive, but you must try to control it intelligently, and only in that way can it be used effectively. I like to use it as a motivational tool. Despite myself, I get angry sometimes, of course. The players say I revert to speaking Italian when I go crazy.

The only thing that really makes me angry is when the attitude of the team is not right. Not the performance – the attitude. I remember one game when we were 2–0 up at half-time. We were comfortable, but I was angry because it didn't matter that we were winning. The attitude was not acceptable – not professional. If we had continued in that way we would have ended up losing, so I got angry with the team to let them know what I thought, and they went out and played well. We scored early and everything was easy from then on.

The attitude is key, even if you're winning. You cannot always control the result, but you can control your attitude, and this is why it makes me angry. On some days you might be able to have a bad attitude and win, or a good attitude and lose, but you're going to win more games with the better attitude.

I tend not to get angry when players make mistakes. They might miss penalties or make errors in the game, which can be disappointing, but it happens. If the attitude is right, then OK, put it behind you and move on. However, players being disrespectful or behaving unprofessionally – these are signs of the wrong attitude and this makes me angry. I refuse to accept it and the players should not accept it from one of their teammates. The players remember the occasions when I get angry because it happens rarely. If I was to get angry every single day, they would not remember and it would not be effective on them.

Even after that infamous night in Istanbul, in the Champions League final against Liverpool that we lost, it was not right to be angry because the attitude had been perfect. The quality of the game we played on that day was the best I've coached in a final. It is a prime example of how a manager can control almost all aspects of the game – strategy, tactics, motivation, the opposition team – but the only thing you cannot control is the final score. There is a randomness in football, in life, which you cannot eliminate from any analysis of the game. Over time, however, you can do everything in your power to eliminate as much of the noise in the system as possible.

Of course, I cannot say that it was not a massive disappointment to lose the final but, looking back with the gift of hindsight, I would not have done anything differently. Everyone thinks that we stopped playing after the first half, but it's not true. We played well – even in extra time. Liverpool played well for six minutes out of a hundred and twenty and Milan played well for a hundred and fourteen minutes. When the first Liverpool goal went in we were playing so well that I thought we would score even more goals; after the second I thought about making a change to strengthen our defence but the third goal went in so quickly that we did not get the chance. After that crazy six minutes we dominated the play again and we could have scored several times. Even in extra time we could and should have scored more, but it was not to be.

The atmosphere in the club was solid – the president and

Galliani, they never had a doubt about us. The club pro-tected me and were very supportive from above. Everybody was hurting, though, funnily enough, not so much the play-ers. Not because they do not care, but because it was the last game of the season and they went off on their holidays where they could deal with the disappointment in their own ways. When we came back for the next season we had a fresh start, and that result, rather than create poor morale, was a motivator for us. I'm sure that defeat helped us win the Champions League in 2007, when we faced Liverpool again in the final.

Listen and Learn

Listening is an often overlooked skill. Listening to what other people have to say – my staff, players, general director and those outside the game – and absorbing it, acting upon it or opening up a dialogue about it is something I very much believe is essential for those who wish to lead.

As I've mentioned earlier, I have a lot of discussions with my support staff and listen to and take on their ideas and opinions. Ideas can come from anywhere, so you should always listen to people. It is very important for me to listen to the players. When preparing for some games, you can give an idea to a player and you have to listen to what they think about it. This happened when I thought of playing Sergio Ramos in midfield.

Everyone said, 'How? Why?' But we had been suffering because of injuries to the team and I knew that we had been vulnerable in the air. Playing Ramos in midfield protected the back four and gave me another strong player to defend set plays, along with the centre backs Pepe and Raphaël Varane. It also meant Ramos would be able to win long balls in the air in front of the defenders. Before I implemented this idea, I spoke with Ramos. I didn't tell anybody else except Paul Clement – nobody knew that I had the idea. I spoke with Ramos and he agreed to do it. We didn't even practise it, so that nobody would know what was happening – I wanted it to remain a secret. The important thing was that I listened carefully to Sergio when we discussed it. If he had said he wasn't comfortable doing it, or had suggested as much when we talked, then we would not have done it.

With the team, it is the same. Before some games against Barcelona I would have an idea about how to play, but, before I explain my idea to the players, I want to know what they think. If we have the same idea, no problem, we can go, but if we have different ideas then I have to manage this. I would either change or adapt my idea, or explain it more clearly, emphasizing the positives. At the end, we must all be working towards the same goal. I have no problem about taking the time to explain, but if we have different ideas then I have to convince them that my idea is better than theirs. Of course, they can also convince me. It must be a two-way conversation. That is the power of listening.

I like to think that I can listen well to what the players

need. I do not pry, especially in their lives outside of the club, but I will listen. There are some players who will want to discuss their personal problems and there are those who don't. Either way is OK – I don't want to force anyone if they're not comfortable. This is a personal relationship and it can only work if the player has trust. At Chelsea, I know players like John Terry and Ashley Cole confided in me about such matters because they trusted me. They felt comfortable speaking about personal things, but if the player doesn't have trust, I don't want to force them into it. In the case of someone like John Terry, when he did tell me about things going on in his personal life it made it easier for me to manage the situation. I don't think there were any specific moments when I learned how best to respond in such situations. It comes gradually, with experience. Life teaches us about these things as we get older.

This is an important idea too. As we grow and gain experience, we should never stop learning. My players, staff, family, the culture, language – there is so much around me that I can learn from, and a good leader must never stand still. In fact, we can't afford to, especially considering how quickly the football environment can change. It is vital, too, that the players see that I am also learning. Firstly, and most importantly, you have to want to learn. I actually find I learn mostly from my own team. What can I do with my players, with our style of play? Can I change something? I will either test something out and learn in that way, or I will listen to the players and learn from their responses. A theory might look good on paper, but there are some things that you cannot learn through study – that you must learn by *doing*.

Similarly, you must learn from your experiences. 'Experiential learning', as people like to call it. We were used to playing 4-3-3 in my first year in Madrid, but when we played against Bayern Munich I realized in the first leg, just from watching the team, that this was not the best system to beat them. We needed to do something different. So, next time, we played differently. In training I often try something new and, completely by accident, find the one new thing that will make the difference.

Of course, you cannot be too radical during the season – it should just be fine-tuning. Preseason is different, that is the time to try new things. Above all, when you arrive and meet a new team you don't know the characteristics of the players, but you listen, you learn, you try new things and eventually you reach a solution. I always think that 4-4-2 is the easiest system for the players to understand. It is, therefore, a good place to start with a new team – but from there, who knows?

Preparation

As I look forward to a new challenge at Bayern Munich in the 2016–17 season, it seems like a good moment to look at the kind of preparation I do when I start a new job. The most important thing for me with any new organization is to familiarize myself with the individual characteristics of the players and staff and to consult with as many people as possible about their personalities. Can I meet the outgoing manager? Can I speak with the senior management at the new club? Can I talk to players I know already? Any intelligence I gather that will help me before I meet the players and staff for the first time can only add value. Once I have an outline idea of the playing and coaching staff, I can then concentrate on devising the different formations and methods that will capitalize on these characteristics.

The culture, of course, is important. At this stage I am talking about this from the outside, based upon my conversations with management, but my impression of Bayern is of a club of complete professionalism. It is well organized and run by ex-players and people who understand the game and have always lived it. At Bayern there is a wealth of knowledge of the game that may be unmatched in world football. These are all people who have achieved great things at every level of the game, as players, coaches, administrators and managers.

It is some of these people with whom I will be 'managing up', of course, and part of starting any job is seeing how the hierarchy operates in the organization and meeting those you will be working with. Thanks to my experience with Berlusconi, Abramovich and Pérez, I have served an apprenticeship, so there is very little that can surprise me at any club. At Bayern, they are experienced football people and, as they have chosen me, they know how I work.

The single most exciting aspect of starting any new job for me is meeting the players, and Bayern will certainly be no exception. How will they respond to me after having such great managers before me? How will my ideas be accepted or challenged? The building of individual and group relationships is at the heart of the job, and luckily for me it is a part of the job that I enjoy.

An important thing to address before starting work is to look at the support staff and see if the existing infrastructure is complete, or whether I will need to augment it with some of my own staff. As I've mentioned, after Chelsea I have learned the importance of working with the existing staff and building new loyalties. At Bayern, I will work with their staff and possibly bring some of my own. Integrating these people may be a challenge, but they are all professionals and I don't predict problems.

When starting at a new club, I look at the team's current identity on the pitch, their style of play, and work out if it is allied to my own, or if I will need to adapt to fit with the club. In some jobs in the past there has been a brief to change the style, to make it closer to the club's traditions. Currently Bayern's identity is closely aligned to Guardiola's style – controlling the match through possession. This is not my personal obsession, but I must be careful not to destabilize a winning structure and style. This is another challenge that I am excited to accept. I came to Madrid after Mourinho and he too had a different style from me, but I think I made it work. I feel sure I can do the same at Bayern.

RESPONSIBILITY: THE QUIET WAY

- A member of your organization being *engaged* is not enough; they have to be *aligned* with your wider goals as well. Neither is sufficient by itself.
- Patience is not always a virtue; don't wait too long to make a difficult decision.
- Encourage a learning culture; make it two-way, listen and learn.
- Soft power is the most effective. Dictatorships don't last.
- Try not to get angry very often; it works best if it rarely happens. Pick your moments for maximum effect and then quickly return to calmness.
- You cannot allow setbacks to be the end; recalibrate and start again. Embrace setbacks and your flexibility to adapt as a competitive advantage.
- Get angry only for the things that really matter: lack of work ethic / application and violation of the culture and values of the group.

- With great talent and Gen Y talent the use of power has to be measured. All top talent wants to be told the direction they are heading but they want to be active in driving the vehicle that gets everyone there.

IN THEIR OWN WORDS . . .
THE LIEUTENANT

PAUL CLEMENT ON CARLO

I'm sometimes asked whether there are any non-negotiables with Carlo and it's a hard question: he builds such strong relationships with people that almost everything feels like it's negotiable. He has such a fantastic relationship with the players, built on total respect. He puts himself on the same level as them, wanting feedback from them and wanting to help them and guide them. However, one of the things he is very strong about is what he calls 'bad attitude' – being unprofessional.

He always wanted things done to a high standard, from the way we travelled to the way we played, trained and conducted ourselves. Everything had to be done correctly and everyone had to behave correctly. Oddly enough, he wasn't as worried about how they behaved outside the club as I would have been; he was quite tolerant about that because he used to say that he had no control over it.

Another thing that annoyed him was if any of the players were disrespectful to the backroom staff. On the day before one away game, Carlo wanted to do a brief bit of tactical work. He had already announced the team for the game and he had organized an eleven-a-side practice session with the team against the rest of the squad – the substitutes and those who were going to be left out. He was leading the exercise, I was in the middle of the pitch with the balls, ready to keep the session moving, and Ray Wilkins was on the far side of the field.

José Bosingwa was playing right back for effectively the 'second' team. Ashley Cole and, I think, Florent Malouda were on the left side for the first team and they were able to skip past Bosingwa like he wasn't even there. He just wasn't carrying out his job properly, clearly showing that he was disappointed not to be playing the next day. He had effectively downed tools. I reminded him about the importance of being professional, saying, 'We have a game tomorrow that *everyone* has to prepare properly for, whether you're starting or not,' and he came back at me quite strongly and disrespectfully. I continued talking to him and in the end a couple of people had to jump in between us, including Didier Drogba and Carlo. Not to stop a physical confrontation, you understand, but certainly a verbal one.

Carlo defused the situation and the practice continued, with Bosingwa's attitude not much better. I was fuming afterwards. How could a player react like that when he hadn't been doing his job properly? Later that evening at the team hotel Carlo spoke about the incident to the group, telling them that it was unacceptable. He said that he would not allow that kind of thing to occur again and he very publicly made sure Bosingwa was aware of it. We moved forward from that.

Carlo could be strong when he believed that someone had acted incorrectly. In the six years I worked with him he maintained a very controlled demeanour, and he dealt with the facts and gave solutions. He was excellent at mastering his emotions, though there was one game, when we were at Paris Saint-Germain, where he did go to a level that I'd not seen before. We were playing Evian away and we were really poor. In the dressing room after the game Carlo struck the door so hard as he entered that I was concerned about his arm, not the door, as I followed him in and the players looked up. There was a box on the floor in the middle of the room and he struck it and it hit Ibra on the head. I thought, 'Oh, no,' but to be fair to Zlatan, he just took it, with the straightest face ever. Carlo then went into a rant at the players, very strong and emotional. That was the only time in six years that I saw him like that.

I saw him launch into Italian a few times, which was always a sign that he was angry. Usually everybody would just be quiet and keep their heads down because they didn't have a clue what he was on about. In Paris there were some Italian speakers in the dressing room, so it would make some sense to them. I think saying it in Italian helped him to get the emotion across, as it's very difficult to do this in your second or third language. I don't remember him doing this as much at Chelsea as he did in Paris.

Carlo was excellent at half-time. The dressing room can be a highly charged place then, especially if the game is close or if you're losing. He would use the period to help the players. A few times he was so angry he felt he needed to have an immediate impact. But usually he would initially move into another area to collect his thoughts. During that period the players would be coming down a bit, getting some recovery and talking among themselves. He would listen to me and the other assistants, take that in, and maybe there would be a bit of a dialogue between us.

Carlo would then go back into the main dressing room and deal with the facts. 'All right, they're doing that, we need to do this,' he might say, and he would put it up on the tactics board to make it visual. He would make it clear, with just two or three points, no more than that. There was no waffle, no clichés like, 'Come on, we've got to get stuck in more!' It was all to do with the tactics. Altering the positioning of players or exploiting something he had seen in the opposition, or maybe pointing out what had been working well for us and emphasizing the need to keep that going.

Carlo saw the dressing room as a combination of a sanctuary for the players and the place where he did his work. He would take himself away from it when necessary and he would think, 'I've done my bit now – the training, the video analysis, the team talk, the tactics – now I'm going to step away from it.' When the players were getting changed and ready to go out to warm up he would often just go off and be on his own, maybe play a game like solitaire on his phone. Now that I've been a manager myself, I can see that he did that to disengage. He would leave me and the assistants in the dressing room to do little one-on-ones with the players about things we had discussed earlier. He might say, 'Paul, have a quiet word with this player and make sure they understand their job today.'

When the team sheets were exchanged we'd get together again with the opposition's line-up. We would discuss who was playing, the formation they were likely to use, and work out who would mark whom at set plays. I'd go and put that up on the board and then he would go back to what he was doing, just whiling away the time until the final minutes before the match. We would come back in from the warm-up and he would have a presence again. He would be giving reminders to people and we'd have a huddle, then out we'd go. I think he got that balance right, of taking himself out of it all, both for himself and for the players, and then getting back into it at the right time.

Carlo was committed to shielding the players from the 'presidential noise' above him. Instead he used the staff as a sounding board – he would tell me what was going on upstairs all the time. That's why he puts such store in being able to trust you. If he can, he will be totally loyal.

He wouldn't allow that noise anywhere near the players. Even when the suits wanted to speak to the players, which was usually because they weren't happy about something, he would be there for it and then afterwards he would gather the players together and say, 'This is about us. This is what we need to do – we stay together.'

Carlo's biggest strength is his ability to deal with pressure. At Derby County there are 33,000 fans at home games and you certainly feel the heat as a number one – not only from the fans, but from the media, from ownership and the pressure that you put yourself under. You feel the pressure to win, all the time.

Now, Carlo was dealing with all this at the very highest level – the biggest clubs in the world where the media spotlight, the intensity and the expectation are in another stratosphere. His ability to handle it all is amazing. When you're a number two, you're helping the manager, you don't feel it in the same way because he's the one making the big decisions, he's the one who's accountable. You help him the best you can and you try to show empathy for his position.

As the years went by, Carlo and I became closer and he became more confident in me and trusted me more. It was one of the reasons I enjoyed working with him so much. He made you feel involved, and that's a big thing about human nature, isn't it? You want to feel your contribution is valued. He gave that to me.

He would involve all the assistants; it was just done naturally. He'd ask, 'What do you think about training today. Have you got ideas?' Or, 'What would your team be for the weekend?' Or he'd tell me his idea and ask me whether I agreed, or whether I would go with something else. These kinds of conversations were happening every day, so everybody felt part of the process. You never felt that things were imposed.

My favourite story about this side of Carlo was prior to the FA Cup final against Portsmouth. He put the responsibility to come up with the tactics totally on the team. I wrote it up on the board as the players were saying it and – Bam! – That was the team talk and we went and won the FA Cup.

Carlo has so many qualities, being patient and calm ranking

highly among them. His patience could be seen as both a strength and, to some, a weakness, and, while it's served him well in many situations, there were one or two occasions when I thought he might have been a bit *too* patient.

I was, however, always impressed by his ability to keep everything in perspective, no matter how bad things got, and to retain dignity and integrity. During Carlo's second year at Chelsea we were struggling. It was not looking like we were going to win anything unless we could progress past Manchester United in the quarter-finals of the Champions League. We lost the first game, so there was a lot riding on the second leg, away at Old Trafford; we lost that too and we were eliminated from the competition. When we got back to the dressing room at the end of the match, Mr Abramovich was there on his own waiting for us.

Everybody sat down and there was a period of silence. A lot of people started looking down at the floor to find the answers that weren't there and there was plenty of looking around at each other, wondering what was coming. Some of the other suits arrived, including Ron Gourlay, the chief executive, but there was silence in the room for what felt like an eternity. People started to feel uncomfortable, looking around, thinking, 'Is someone going to say something? Is the owner going to speak? The CEO? Are they waiting for the manager to say something?'

Eventually, a signal was given by Abramovich to Ron Gourlay that someone needed to speak. The chief executive looked a bit sheepish, so Carlo did the honourable thing and took the responsibility. I can't remember his exact words because it was so tense and emotions were running high; the best thing to do would have been to get changed and get out of there. But Carlo couldn't do that. He was forced to say something and it was very difficult. It seemed to go on and on – it felt like we were in there for ever. It was a memorable-for-the-wrong-reasons moment.

Perhaps I would have stayed working at youth level if it weren't for Carlo. Only by his inspiration and motivation was I given the chance to operate at the highest level, which is what we all want to do, whatever sphere we're in. After my initial 'loan' spell with the first-team squad, I told him it was perhaps time for me to go back to the academy because I wasn't sure I was ready for the first team. He wouldn't have any of it. 'Of course you're ready,' he said. 'You stay with me.'

His endorsement enabled me to make that step up. He's been the single biggest influence on me as a coach and as a person. We keep in contact regularly, on the phone and texting each other all the time.

When he arrived at Chelsea he was an icon in European and world football, and that was intimidating at the start. But as soon as you get to know him you realize he's a lovely guy, humble. There is no doubt that Carlo is a special person. He judges everybody on their merits. Nobody is better or worse than anybody else in his eyes; everybody has value. He cares about people – his players and his staff.

7. The Product

Every business has at its heart the delivery of the product to the consumer. In football that product is on the pitch. What happens there drives the three basic revenue streams of the business: match day (ticket sales), commercial (sales and sponsorship) and broadcasting (which dominates the turnover of most of the elite European football leagues). So, ultimately, despite the importance of everything else to the business, I will be judged on the game and delivering success. Of course, success at the big clubs means trophies; at smaller clubs it could mean avoiding relegation or simply staying in business.

Identity

The key to everything on the field is the identity of the team. What I mean here by identity is the style of your play, what is seen on the pitch. Are you defensive? What are your views on possession? What do you do when you have control of the ball? These are the factors that create the identity of the team. I do not think of my own identity, but only that of the team, and this depends on what the club asks of you, the characteristics of the players and the history and tradition of the club.

Real Madrid has a very clear identity that is rooted in its history and traditions. In the ten years from 1956 they won six European Cups, five in a row, playing in a certain way, and that is part of the DNA of the club. This was one of the reasons why 'La Décima' was so important. They like to have attacking football. The fans expect it and the president has to honour that.

When you arrive at a club, you want to introduce some change to re-motivate the players and to announce yourself and your views, but you don't want to fundamentally change the identity. There was little difference in identity between the way Milan played and the identity that was being developed at Paris Saint-Germain: possession of the ball, finding space between the lines. So, instead, when I joined each of these teams I changed a lot of the training sessions while keeping the same identity. The players would do different exercises from before and we generally mixed things up to keep the attention of the players. When you are proposing something new the players are more motivated to listen and work. They concentrate more in training, which helps me in the job, especially in the beginning.

The maintenance of an identity was the problem Louis van Gaal faced when he arrived at Manchester United and it was the same for David Moyes before him. Manchester

United's identity, like Real Madrid's, is to attack – for United it is to attack with power and pace. Of course, if they continue to win that will be accepted, but when things begin to get difficult the identity will become an issue. This is a problem at Madrid even if you are winning. Fabio Capello was sacked after winning La Liga and for Mourinho it ended the same way.

All of this was also a problem for me when I arrived at Madrid. The players had been asked to play in what was seen as a non-Madrid way before me, with more counter-attacking football. In my opinion, the players were not the problem. My job was to allow them to play the Madrid way. Of course it helped that we were able to recruit more players who fitted the club's core identity. This was what the president wanted too, which always makes it easier.

We signed Gareth Bale from Tottenham and Isco from Malaga. Bale was just a special talent that any team would want. I wanted Isco because he is a talented player but also a hard worker; I believed he could become an important long-term player for Madrid. Once the players were all in place, I could change the system to suit the type of the players at my disposal, so that we would have more control of the ball. I made some changes, putting Di María in midfield.

For the start of my second season, we were able to get Toni Kroos from Bayern Munich, who is exactly the type of player that fits the identity of Madrid. He is very precise – perfect to build play from the back. I didn't want to lose Xabi Alonso because I thought he and Kroos could play together. Previously, we had played Luka Modrić and Alonso together. When Modrić got injured during the season we went through a bad time because, with no Alonso, there was no ideal replacement. German midfielder Sami Khedira was out with a long-term injury, so I had to try different things, like playing Ramos with Kroos, and it could not be the same. Ramos played really well, but he is not a natural midfielder like Modrić or Alonso.

When we lost Karim Benzema to injury that season it meant that the centre of our identity was lost. We had to play 4-4-2 instead of 4-3-3, with Ronaldo and Bale up front. Ramos was also not fit but he was there – because he is Ramos. People only see Benzema as a striker but he also has the skills of a clever midfielder. He's everything – a fantastic all-round footballer. He linked our play, so when he was missing it damaged our identity.

I am often asked why Real Madrid hired Mourinho. The answer is easy: They wanted to beat Barcelona. At that time Mourinho was the best manager in Europe.

Forget tradition? Of course – winning is the best tradition of all. Aligning with the identity and culture of the club will not be enough if you don't win. In my last season we played attacking football and scored over 150 goals. We followed the tradition, the history of the club – but ultimately it didn't matter. Ultimately, if you don't win trophies you get sacked.

The identity has to come from the head coach but it cannot override the club. The tradition and brand of the club are massively important. Each manager has their own way they like to play, and any club hiring them must accept that they will bring this approach with them. When you hire a Guardiola or a Wenger, you are buying into a specific approach to the game. Their obsession is that style – playing with a lot of possession – will drive results. If it's a Ferguson or a Mourinho, you are buying into a different approach. Winning is the aim, and that will drive the style.

A winning culture is something that all clubs want to have. Most might be proud of their identity, but they would sacrifice it straight away just to win. Of course, there are exceptions like Barça and, strangely enough, West Ham United in England. When Sam Allardyce was their manager, he was challenged about the club's style, the famous West Ham way, and he would say that West Ham had a false image of themselves – that the 'West Ham way' seemed to be 'not winning'. In the end, even though Allardyce won promotion to the Premier League and did well there, even though he delivered everything that was asked of him by the owners, he still got the sack, because he was anti-culture. Slaven Bilić was then hired to deliver success the West Ham way and, so far, it seems to be working well.

Whenever my Chelsea team played Sir Alex's Manchester United it was easy to see a clear identity. That identity of the team perfectly matched the brand of the club; the manager and owners were in unison. They tried to play the same way every time – same style, same attitude, same intensity. This was partly because Sir Alex built not only a team, but an infrastructure, from top to bottom – he built everything. I saw a real sense of belonging in everybody around the club. It reminded me of my time at Milan, this feeling of family and tradition again. At Chelsea you could see a similar sense of belonging in people like John Terry and Frank Lampard. Perhaps this is why clubs often appoint their ex-players – they believe they will naturally be part of the family.

That was definitely why I was appointed at Reggiana and Milan. Of course, it doesn't mean that you will be successful – we have seen many ex-players fail badly – but it enables a quick entry and understanding of the organization and identity. If you look at Diego Simeone's success at Atlético Madrid, it is partly due to his relationship with the fans and the club as a player. But he still had to deliver results, which he has done brilliantly, and with a very specific identity. This was an example of picking the head coach to fit with and maintain the culture of the club and match the identity of the team to that culture. If Atlético had wanted to change the identity, then maybe Simeone would not have been the correct appointment.

After Sir Matt Busby at Manchester United, several managers had a go at the job but none was so successful until Sir Alex came along. It wasn't until Sir Alex that the true identity of the club could be re-established, which, along with the trophies, of course, helped him stay a long time. Busby had been manager for twenty-four years and his first replacement didn't last a year – a similar situation to David Moyes after Sir Alex. Sadly, in today's game it seems that these types of long-term managers, who provide success as well as maintaining the identity and tradition of the club, are unlikely to be seen again.

Tactics

Although the overall identity of the team, the style of play, is very important, it is perhaps best understood as strategic. The tactics – how to perform in particular games or particular periods of the season, or how to change systems or personnel against particular opponents – are also crucial to success.

When people talk about football they often seem to believe that to play 'offensively' is good and to play 'defensively' is bad. That's not true. If you have a team that plays well defensively but not so well offensively, or the other way round, that is the sign of a bad manager. You must be strong when either attacking or defending. In Italian football, the tradition and history of the game are defensive: *catenaccio*, a defensive system of play, was born in Italy to an Argentine, Helenio Herrera.

Attacking play is more about the creative qualities of the players, but defensive play is different. Anybody and everybody can learn to defend well. If they don't it is because either the manager allows it to happen or the players choose not to defend well. Great defensive play is mostly organizational and positional in the modern game – it's not so much about tackling any more. It's all about concentration. Of course, you have to be physically conditioned, you have to run and sacrifice. Players don't like it when they don't have the ball. Nobody likes to run without the ball – they all want to run with it.

This is where systems become important. As I've said, when I was starting out I was wedded to 4-4-2. I have now learned to be more flexible although I still believe that 4-4-2 is the outstanding defensive system. You have the best coverage of the pitch, it is simpler to press forward and press high, with coverage behind the pressing players. With 4-3-3, for example, although you can press high because you have three strikers, it can expose limitations in midfield behind those forwards, especially on the flanks. Also, if your forwards are not great at defending it can be easier for defenders to bypass them and get into the next line with superior numbers. This is less likely with 4-4-2, where you can bring in the wide players to bolster the midfield so that your central players are not overwhelmed.

There is, of course, a downside that can be exposed in 4-4-2. When you are attacking you have to use a lot more lateral passes to get forward and then deliver into the scoring zone, whereas with 4-3-3 you can move the ball through the lines quicker and attack more centrally. Perhaps the ultimate will be the Guardiola vision of eleven midfielders – even the goalkeeper. This is not so crazy, because if you play with a high line then the goalkeeper has to be fast and competent with his feet, like Manuel Neuer at Bayern Munich or Hugo Lloris at Tottenham.

When I hear other coaches saying that their team was outnumbered in midfield, I say, 'Look, we've got to stop thinking like this because we've got eleven players on the field and they've got eleven – if we're outnumbered somewhere, they must be outnumbered somewhere else on the field. Let's concentrate on playing in these areas.'

In the military, they say that no strategy survives contact with the enemy. This is so true in football. You plan all week and then the opponent chooses different players from those you had thought he would or, as soon as the game starts, you realize that they are using a different system to the one you had planned for. Or, for specific matches, where the opponent always plays the same way but your team struggles against them, you might have to change formation to fit the opposition.

In my time at Real we had difficulties with our local rivals Atlético. They always played the same, but were always difficult. When we played them we had to counter what they wanted to do. Their strength was in the middle of the pitch, where they were very aggressive. When they won the ball they would immediately use it to attack. So, our tactics for the games were not to use the middle of the pitch, but to use the flanks to put in crosses quickly. I also made the full backs play really high up the pitch to press the ball quickly when we lost it to deny them any possibility of counter-attacking.

You often have to change formation to work around injured players or to accommodate new ones. Sometimes this is where the best ideas come from – from constraints. At Milan, we had a lot of quality players arrive and at first I was struggling to fit them all in the team and keep them happy, but then we stumbled upon a beautiful accident. First, Andriy Shevchenko picked up an injury, so I moved Andrea Pirlo back to a deeper role, as playmaker behind the two offensive midfielders. We ended up inventing the Christmas tree formation. It came about as a practical necessity but it married perfectly to the philosophy of the president. As they say in England, 'Necessity is the mother of invention.'

The key to the success of the Christmas tree formation came in one game, against Deportivo de La Coruña in the Champions League. They had two deep-lying midfielders and I thought that playing with our normal team, minus our injured players, we would not be able to defensively cover the position of these players. They would be too deep for us to affect. So, instead we played two offensive midfield players who could push up on them when we didn't have the ball. You could say that the whole idea was, in fact, born of thinking not offensively, but defensively, which you might say is typically Italian. 'How could we stop the opposition?' was first in my thoughts. We won the match 4–0. Maybe if we had lost 4–0 I would have discarded the idea altogether. In our next game in the Champions League we played against Bayern Munich and we won again, 2–1, with the formation, so I started to believe that I was necessity's child.

In football, as in anything, you must never stand still.

Never believe that the tactics you deploy today and that have brought you great success will continue to be effective tomorrow. Your opponents will not be sitting back and letting it happen again. Look at the Chelsea team in the 2015–16 season. The season before, they were champions and all but invulnerable; then, suddenly, they can hardly win a game. It's the same players, tactics and system, so what's changed? The difference is that other teams have moved on and worked out how to play the Chelsea system.

To stand still can actually mean to go backwards. I like tennis and each time I see a new type of player emerge – Chris Evert, Martina Navratilova, Steffi Graf, Serena Williams, Björn Borg, Andre Agassi, Pete Sampras, Roger Federer, Novak Djokovic – I can never believe they will be beaten. But they always are. When I was talking with Billy Beane, of the Oakland Athletics baseball team and *Moneyball* fame, he said that his revolutionary practices gave him an edge for maybe one year and then everyone else copied and improved.

Foot Soldiers

The players that others refer to as the foot soldiers, the workhorses or the 'water carriers' – they are the ones to whom I'm closest. This kind of player has the character I value the most, because when I played, I had more or less the same skill, the same ability as they have.

The foot soldiers are the players who give their heart for the team – every time, in every game and training session – so I don't need to spend a lot of time with these kind of players. They are the low-maintenance team members who allow you the time to spend on the high-maintenance ones. They self-motivate 100 per cent of the time.

I remember all these players as much as the superstars, because without them there *are* no superstars. It's a cliché, but it really is a team game. At Reggiana, for example, the hardest worker in midfield was Leonardo Calucci, while at Parma I had Roberto Sensini. With Juventus it was Antonio Conte or Edgar Davids, who had a lot of personality. These were players who were also stars, but they had a soldier's mentality, and sometimes it was easy to forget their talent and needs.

The first time I met Davids I told him, 'I'm happy to be your manager because you are fantastic. You are strong and aggressive – you are always giving 100 per cent.' He looked at me and said, 'I am also a talented football player.' I had made the classic mistake of assuming that great players do not work hard. These players are sometimes not recognized by the fans and the owners, but they are by those who lead them.

At Chelsea the soldiers were Branislav Ivanović and John Terry, at Paris Saint-Germain it was Alex and at Madrid the soldier was, in my last year, Toni Kroos. I had Gennaro Gattuso at Milan and I also had Clarence Seedorf. People do not see him as a soldier but he is very strong.

Seedorf is a player that you have to delegate things to.

You have to tell him, 'Take care of this,' and he will do it, but if you are not specific he has such a strong personality that he will want to do everything. The key was to move him to where I thought he would have most value, and I had to convince him of that.

When he arrived at Milan in 2002 Seedorf fought a lot with his teammates. He's such a strong character that he was behaving like he was in charge of the other players. Eventually, they said to him, 'You are not the manager – you don't have to talk like this.' The reality was that Seedorf could be the soldier *and* the leader, but Paolo Maldini was the leader in the dressing room, so we had to create a balance to get the best from Seedorf. What he was doing was not intended to be bad – he was just overexcited and passionate about how to play. He had interesting ideas but he was too forceful when explaining them to the others. We had to find the way in between. I told Seedorf that he had to be more polite and patient when explaining certain things and to the others I said that they had to understand he had my confidence in what he was doing. I would say to Seedorf, 'This is a good idea, but a bad way to convince people. We have to educate the other players more slowly.'

Seedorf is one of those players I always want in my team. Ultimately, this kind of player is a reference point to his teammates. Leaders are chosen by the group, not the manager or the president, and, in the end, Seedorf was a leader. He learned to tone things down and the players wanted his personality and his confidence in the group. Character is often more important than technique.

The Opposition

In the top level of global football there are a very small cadre of top managers and I have been privileged to compete against them all at various stages of my career. Knowing how they work and how their teams play is essential for me when my teams play against theirs – but it is also important so that I can learn from them.

I am asked about other managers a lot but I don't necessarily know them personally, so I can only really talk about their teams and how they play. Of course, you could argue, as many do, that their teams reflect the mentality and personality of the manager. For example, Arsène Wenger's teams will always be attacking, but on a sliding scale. As attacking as the 'Invincibles' were in 2003–04, they were also very strong when not in possession, with Patrick Vieira in the centre of midfield in front of Sol Campbell and Kolo Touré at the back. They were big – close to three centimetres taller on average than the current team. Like they say in boxing, a good big 'un will always beat a good little 'un. Can this be Wenger constantly trying to achieve the perfect attacking balance? Is that who he is? Certainly, his teams seem to reflect that.

When I play against teams like Arsenal that like to have

the ball, you have to be tough. You have to be stronger in the challenges and you must be patient and not too afraid when they have the ball, because that could actually be to your advantage on the counter-attack.

José Mourinho's style is different. He doesn't like to concede anything. Mourinho will stay o–o for a long time and be waiting, waiting. He's not worried about it staying o–o. Again, the analogy is boxing – his team plays like a counter-punching fighter. He's prepared to go eleven rounds to tire you out, so he can knock you out in the twelfth round. His teams will work you to death and then, when you're tired, he'll go in for the kill.

With Pep Guardiola, you know that possession is key for him. His team will have the ball and you know this and must accept it. You can't compete against Guardiola's teams in terms of possession, but this is not all bad. When you don't have possession, you have fewer problems to solve. When you have the ball, you have more problems because there is more complexity in creating than in destroying. Destroying is easier, it is about organization and discipline and anybody can be taught this. Creativity is more difficult to teach.

When we prepared for the Champions League semi-final first leg against Bayern Munich, everyone at Real Madrid was worried about the possession of Bayern. They had beaten Barcelona convincingly the season before, so we knew they would be strong. In the meetings before the game, I concentrated on convincing my players that our opponents' possession was actually key to us winning the game. I told the players not to worry if Bayern had a lot of possession at the start, because we could gradually work our own game in and control without the ball, as long as we stayed calm and were always in position. It was vital not to lose position. In the first twenty minutes of the match we barely touched the ball, though we somehow managed to score. I tried to get a message on to say that we could worry a little bit if we didn't touch it again for the next twenty minutes. At half-time I said, 'OK, I didn't mean don't worry *at all*.'

With Sir Alex Ferguson's teams the game is always open. The key against Manchester United was to understand that what was important for them was not so much the tactics, but the rhythm of the game – the power, speed and intensity. Of course, Ferguson developed tactically over his time at United, and he learned to be very effective in the Champions League. If you played against a Ferguson team, you knew you must try to disrupt.

Diego Simeone is very similar to Mourinho. In Spain, his style of play is to be passionate, aggressive, strong rhythm and with team spirit.

All managers have their own way, their own style, but for me it pays to be flexible. I need to have some room to adjust – some elasticity. For others, this is not their way. One of the coaches I most admired was the Ukrainian Valeriy Lobanovskyi. He had no elasticity at all outside of his system. Within the system, he would say, anything is permitted; outside of the system, nothing is permitted. For him it fitted that there could be flexibility in discussing the system and discussing how they were going to play – but once the decision had been made, that would be final. If the plan was to commit five midfield players forward on the understanding that the ball would be played into a certain position, then it was unacceptable to him for the ball to be played anywhere else.

I once watched a training session run by Lobanovskyi when I was a player with Roma and the sheer intensity was unbelievable. He would use the whole length of the pitch, playing with three groups of seven. The first two groups would play attack against defence and when the defending team won the ball, they had to pass and move through midfield and play against the other seven. He played like this for forty-five minutes, repeating the exercise over and over again. I tried it at Madrid and the players managed only fifteen minutes. It was crazy.

Lobanovskyi's Dynamo Kiev teams didn't have many great individuals – they had Oleh Blokhin, Igor Belanov, Andriy Shevchenko and Serhiy Rebrov at various stages – but it was all about the team. The team always came first. Lobanovskyi's rule was iron – within the system, anything; outside the system, nothing.

THE PRODUCT: THE QUIET WAY

- Know your business. Those you lead expect nothing less. If they observe less, they won't be led by you for long.
- Don't ignore the foot soldiers in an organization just because they're low maintenance.
- Everyone goes through ups and downs; treat even the quiet talent with the same level of concern and consideration as the star talent.
- If you hit upon a great idea by accident, go with it.
- Interview the organization to ensure that you're aligned with the identity they want to create or maintain. Do your due diligence before you agree to join – what is the governance structure, to whom do you report, who reports to you? The answers to these and other questions will be central to your ultimate success or failure.
- Always be thinking about winning; developing a winning mentality across the entire organization is the only way to guarantee success over time.

- Treat every day as if tomorrow is the day your talent will implode. This 'positive paranoia' will force you to understand their dynamic development and anticipate the REAL issues that derail them.
- Let the product / talent breathe on your problems. Include them, encourage them to be active participants in finding a solution. If there is a stalemate on the final direction then the leader has the final decision.
- Remember, there are no great coaches or leaders. They are only as great as the talent they seduce and lead and how much permission this talent gives them on a daily basis to deliver their ideas.

IN THEIR OWN WORDS . . .
THE OPPONENTS

SIR ALEX FERGUSON ON CARLO

My first experience up against Carlo was the 1999 semi-final of the Champions League, when he was coach with Juventus. I didn't really know him at all, but because I was quite friendly with Marcello Lippi I asked him, 'How is the new guy, Ancelotti? Should I have a drink with him?' He said, 'Oh, he's a great guy, but if he comes for a drink after just make sure it's a good one.'

We didn't have that drink. These things happen in a European tie. After the semi-final in Turin, there was so much euphoria in our dressing room at getting to the final for the first time since 1968 that you forget a lot of things. I didn't see him in the end, but then over the years he would pop up in different places. I've always known that his teams were very difficult to beat and that they played with expression.

The one occasion I must talk about – because I thought he behaved with unbelievable dignity – was when he was with Chelsea and he came into my dressing room at Old Trafford after the match. When he sat down, I knew there was something wrong. I thought he might have had some bad family news, but it was Abramovich. When Carlo had returned to the dressing room, Abramovich was waiting because they'd lost. He told Carlo in no uncertain terms what the consequences would be. Carlo was really upset, so I said, 'Just forget it. He can't get rid of you in the middle of the season.'

In retrospect I think Carlo was right to worry. Abramovich had made his mind up. Carlo had taken off Fernando Torres and put Didier Drogba on, who scored right away. Eventually, we won the game 2–1, and the tie 3–1 on aggregate. Abramovich had bought Torres for fifty million pounds. Do you remember that? What a waste of money – an absolute waste of money. But because he had paid all that money out *and* they had lost *and* Carlo had subbed Torres, I think Abramovich had already decided Carlo's fate.

Carlo must have known that he'd get this sort of a death at Chelsea, but he composed himself after. We had a glass of wine and he settled down fine, but he knew the inevitable was going to happen. In his last game he was at Everton and they had a car waiting for him and he never went back to the team. But when he arrived back in London the Chelsea boys – Frank Lampard and the rest – took him out for a farewell dinner, which is brilliant. That's exactly what you'd expect for someone that's played a part in their lives.

We've been friends since that time. He's a gentleman, but a gentleman with a purpose. He has this quiet manner about him, which allows him to really listen. People who know how to listen properly take a lot in. He's not a guy who will dominate the room, but when he does say something, it's always worth hearing.

Carlo is a good man and a great coach. I had hoped that he would come to Manchester United, but it didn't quite work out. Another time, maybe.

8. Data

In sport, as in business, organizations are constantly searching for new ways to gain an advantage over the competition. This competitive edge is invariably sought out in the analytical and the psychological sides of the business. The consensus of opinion in sport seems to be that we 'get' the physical side of the business – we are all more or less on the same lines in the areas of conditioning, training, etc. – but with the data and the mind of the player, there are multiple new approaches, techniques and technology still to be developed.

Of course, we rarely get the future right, but we have to start somewhere. Plans never work out perfectly, but having no plan at all is even worse. It means you have no direction and are forced to be reactive instead of proactive.

Analytics

Statistical analysis can often frighten leaders more used to trusting their own, often instinctive judgements. But ever since *Moneyball* – Michael Lewis's book which traced how the evidence-based, statistical approach of Billy Beane's Oakland Athletics challenged baseball wisdom – the analytics of sport have become more acceptable. They are still threatening to some, however. I know of managers who wilfully ignore the data produced by the analytics departments, but this cannot last for ever. If a club is forced to choose between an entire department they have poured money into as part of a long-term strategy and a manager, it will not be a difficult decision to make.

At Madrid we used statistics mainly for the physical aspects of the players. For me, their most important use is to control the physical elements of training – tiredness, fatigue – so that a potential injury to a player can be avoided. This is what the GPS data does. I know that clubs also use the numbers for recruitment purposes, but I'm not as involved in this and it is not used so much for coaching.

To be honest, even if we receive analytics and data that's saying that the team is deficient in some way, we still don't use it as well as we might. It is my fault as much as anyone's because I'm not convinced that the numbers regarding technical data, by which I mean what the player does with the ball – shooting, crossing, heading, passing – has as much value as is claimed. This is another area where I can learn and develop myself. How often do I, as the head coach, ask the analytics guys to find me data, to interrogate the data? The answer is, probably, not very often. We will all need to get better at utilizing all of the data, because if we don't, others certainly will.

It is equally important not to get too carried away with the numbers. They are a tool – they shouldn't become an obsession. At one time it was all about possession, with all the analysts concentrating on that. Why? Because it was something they could measure. But as Albert Einstein reportedly said, 'Not everything that can be counted counts, and not everything that counts can be counted.' Possession alone, of course, doesn't win the game. There is only one piece of data that always correlates with a victory and that is goals. If you score more goals than your opponent, you win.

The technical data is only about the minute or two that the player has the ball. I want the physical data about what he is doing for the other eighty-eight or eighty-nine minutes. I need that for tactical reasons. How quickly can players recover into defensive positions at certain times in the game? If I know this, then I can know how far forward I can commit players and still give them the chance to recover.

If we go back to Arrigo Sacchi, my managerial mentor, and look at the system he played, it is clear that he would have been helped by the physical data showing the amount of work the players do to recover their correct positions in his system. If you play at high intensity, like Jürgen Klopp's teams at Dortmund and now Liverpool, this will also be very important. Here, the question is not, 'Is the system right,' but rather, 'Is it sustainable over a whole season, or two, or three?' Will the players be able to sustain such energy output and the strain on their bodies?

I have people delivering data to me all the time when I'm

managing. At Chelsea, it was Mike Forde and Nick Broad. These were young guys who valued the data. But I also had Giovanni Mauri, who was more old school. He was the necessary counterbalance to the numbers analysis. I have confidence in Mauri *because* he trusts his instincts, which have been acquired through years of experience. We need both analytics and instinct because eventually those who do not understand the data will be eaten by it.

Nick would analyse distances covered and work out if players were more vulnerable to injury. He would tell me that if a player did certain things at a particular time in the game, they would be more likely to score. He would have this information for both our own players and the opposition's. Again, this kind of information, the physical data, would help me make tactical decisions.

At Madrid, before we played Atlético, my analysts told me that on average Diego Costa would run eight kilometres in a game, mostly with long runs at speed, into the space behind the full backs. However, occasionally he would only run half that amount, and in those games Atlético lost. So, tactically, could we stop him making those runs? I told the full backs to drop back and deny him the space behind them and force him to go short to receive the ball at his feet, with his back to goal. We didn't always beat Atlético, but we denied Costa most times.

The data that's most important to me is to watch the game. My best analytical tool is my eyes. I have the knowledge and experience that come from watching thousands of games, and any data I receive from my staff tends to complement that knowledge. That knowledge can also override the data. My job is to see all the data, sift through it and then decide which is relevant. I get my staff to watch the game and provide their own intuitive analysis. I ask them about the opposition, about their organization, recovery of the ball, speed of counter-attack, set plays – everything.

The importance of sifting this data, of not getting carried away with numbers just for the sake of numbers, cannot be overstated. At Chelsea an analyst came to me and said, 'There are three players, Salomon Kalou, Joe Cole and Nicolas Anelka, and when they play together, they run more than one thousand metres without the ball in a sprint. There is a direct correlation with this and winning the game.' 'Great,' I said, 'and where do you suggest we put Drogba?'

The important data is that Ronaldo scores sixty goals in sixty games. This means that, on average, he scores one goal a game – which usually means that when Ronaldo plays you win. Even before the game starts, you're already winning 1–0. The technical data we need to worry about is where these goals originate. If the opposition works this out then we have to react, but the great thing about Ronaldo is that, even if you know what is coming, it is difficult to stop. It's the Lombardi rule. Legendary American football coach Vince Lombardi had fewer plays than other teams and he didn't mind if the others knew what they were. His idea was simply to be as close to perfect as possible on the key plays so that whatever the opposition did, they could not stop them.

Mind Games

The psychological aspect is one of the least exploited in football. The media often like to talk about mind games and psychological 'warfare' that managers might use, to try to influence players and referees, but I am not interested. I am known for not participating in these kinds of tactics and I take pride in behaving respectfully with my players, the club and myself. It is not my style to defame opponents or referees in pursuit of a psychological gain. I fight with my team on the pitch, nowhere else.

I am, however, very interested in using psychology for the good of my players and the team. In my experience we have a lot of knowledge about the physical aspects, but not about the mind. I had a psychologist on the staff at both Chelsea and Milan, but not at Madrid. This aspect of the game is extremely interesting and useful, but one reason it is not widely practised is because the players are resistant. They think it's too personal – too much like going to see a psychiatrist.

In one sense we have always worked on the psychology as much as the physical, just without the science. Every day as a manager you have something psychological to deal with. Keeping players happy, keeping them motivated – it's all psychological. At Madrid I had Marcelo come to tell me that he wanted to play every game. If I did not make this happen then he would go to the president and ask to leave the club.

I said, 'Listen, now is not the moment because the market is closed, so you have to stay here until the end of the season.' He was an experienced player – not old, but experienced – and he was frustrated because he hadn't played in the previous game. Not because he was dropped, but just to rest him.

This is an example of how, when trying to keep your players motivated, you must communicate well with them. There was no reason for him to be alarmed, and with a lack of clear communication he could have thought that it was the club that was not happy with him. I told him, 'When you don't play it can be for two reasons. The first reason is because you played badly and the second reason to give to you a rest. For you, it is the second reason, because I don't want to kill you. I want you to be fresh for the next match. You are too important to have you tired out in this match – so rest.'

Every day there are these psychological issues. They are small to me, but huge for the player. It is also important that my staff understand the issues and that we have the same type of communication with each individual. We must try to help that player understand because we can't always change the situation – sometimes they are just playing badly.

If we look at the game itself, then we can see the importance of psychology. Taking a penalty when you are winning 5–0 with one minute left in the game is different from taking a penalty in the shootout of the final of the World Cup with 100,000 in the stadium and 2 billion watching on TV. At the 1994 World Cup, where I was working as assistant to

Italy manager Arrigo Sacchi, we reached the final, against Brazil, which was settled with a penalty shootout. 'Surely it's impossible for Franco Baresi and Roberto Baggio to miss the goal?' I thought. But not only did they miss the goal, we're still looking for the ball that Baresi hit. It's all in the mind.

During that tournament, Sacchi wanted technical data for the match for the first time. I had guys with computers sitting with me all the time, saying things like 'this many passes for Baggio' or 'Demetrio Albertini's movement without the ball is this' – blah, blah, blah, all the time. We were a goal down and it was late in the game against Nigeria in the first knockout round when I had to put a stop to it and shouted, 'Close the computers and concentrate on what's going on in front of us! If we lose against Nigeria we will not be allowed home again – they will kill us.' We scored a late goal and went on to win 2–1 in extra time. After the match Sacchi asked to see the statistics and I said, 'Of course, but we don't have the whole match – I was more worried about going home early than the statistics.'

He said to me, 'No, no, no – I need ninety minutes, plus the extra time, of course.' So I went upstairs with a video, made an analysis of the rest of the match and Sacchi was happy. But don't tell me statistics won that match for us – the key to winning the game was casting aside the distractions and concentrating on the severity of the situation. It was the psychology, again.

We need to work more on this and we need help from

professionals. The players must understand that it is help, not criticism. For example, neuroscientists are looking at ways of improving the identification of talented individuals – that could be another way to help us. Any edge that we can gain is an edge that can keep us winning . . . and keep us in a job.

DATA: THE QUIET WAY

- Don't try to play 'mind games'. Focus on what's important: results.
- Your most important analytical tools are your eyes and your brain. Draw on your experience and don't get distracted.
- Equally, don't be afraid of data and analytics – embrace new developments and any edge they can give you.
- Create a place at the table for analytics to thrive. Don't treat the theme and person(s) as a 'nice to have' feature. Give it credibility but in return you need them to fully understand the sole reason they are there: to help us to win.
- Embrace data but as a leader your role is to translate it into insight and then be the point person for delivering it to the talent. The leader has the 'emotional credits' with the talent to make the data insights fly on the battlefield.
- Psychology is crucial. The mindset of your colleagues and teams will drive your success. Give people confidence to be themselves.
- Clear communication is vital, especially to explain tough decisions.

IN THEIR OWN WORDS . . .
THE OPPONENTS

ROBERTO MARTÍNEZ ON CARLO

Let me tell you a story about Carlo which shows the kind of guy he is. My wife drove down to Stamford Bridge one day to watch a game and she parked in the car park underneath the stadium. When she tried to start the car after the game, she had the oil warning light come up. As she opened the bonnet to check the oil, a guy came up to her and said, 'Excuse me, have you got a problem?' It was Carlo – I think he was chilling out a bit in the car park – and, in his full Chelsea suit, he rolled up his sleeves and refilled the oil for my wife. He didn't know who she was – he would have done it for anybody. He did that straight after a game, just being himself, helping someone, and I think he manages that way. He tries to help people, to understand them, and he gets the best out of them in the dressing room. There's no secret as to why he's been so successful in high-pressure situations with the big expectations and the big players – it's down to that.

I was managing Wigan when I came up against Carlo in the

Premier League. Everybody was saying how much he had changed the Chelsea mentality and so, of course, I was very pleased that we managed to beat them 3–1 and give Carlo his first defeat in the Premier League. From my point of view, what I immediately thought of the man was, 'Here is a real gentleman.' He struck me as someone with incredible human values, and then you see that he manages that way as well. He puts players with big egos and big personalities into a system, which is the hardest thing to do, and manages to give it a bit of normality.

The other thing I noticed was that, as the game progressed and we scored more goals, he never lost the rag – never lost his composure. I remember that Ray Wilkins, his assistant, was telling him, 'We need to throw John Terry into the box like an extra striker,' and Ancelotti just said, 'Whoa, whoa. We don't do that. We need to be patient and play our way out of this.' Whether he was correct or not wasn't the point; he was under massive pressure but you could see that he was in control and he could make a decision.

Every time we played against him I always found real admiration for such a high-profile manager who was also an old-fashioned manager; he was managing big individuals, trying to understand both the player and the human being, trying to get the best out of them and get the quality in a group. After that first defeat there were little ups and downs and you could see that he always controlled the dynamics in the group, always understood the players and found the right solutions. That was him: never pretending to be someone else, always being himself.

Ancelotti is very clever tactically. In that first game we played, he had the Christmas tree formation, 4-3-2-1, from his time at Milan, and that was something we had to try to break down. I think we surprised Ancelotti in that game. However, in the last game of that season, we had already achieved survival in the Premier League and were playing for nothing – the players already had their suitcases packed in the dressing room. Obviously we were trying to win the game, but the Chelsea players had complete focus as they had to win to be crowned champions, and they did so convincingly.

When we played at Stamford Bridge in his second season, he showed the way that he thinks about the game. We were trying to take advantage of a specific player and he spotted this straight away. We were the better side in the first half, but he changed things, taking John Obi Mikel off and making things very difficult for us, and we ended up losing a tight match. That showed he could read the game well – his tactical disposition was very important.

One of the criticisms that he comes under – I know this happened in Madrid, but also to a certain extent at Paris Saint-Germain and even at Chelsea – is that because he has such a good relationship with the players it can get soft. One of the things he says himself is that he sometimes gets 'lazy', but what he means by this is that he can be too patient – you know, hang on, just that little bit longer. I know exactly that type of relationship. When you trust a player, you accept them making a mistake or their form dropping – you just want to create a bond where you're going to get them back to their level.

But every manager has a different style. Ultimately, everyone is going to judge a manager on results. In football a dangerous kind of logic can creep in. What happens is that if you lose and you're seen as soft, that's pinpointed as the reason why you are losing. If you lose and you're seen as a dictator, that's the reason why you are losing. But if you win and you're soft, that's the reason you're winning.

You could say that Real Madrid in December 2014 under Ancelotti were at the best level a Madrid team has ever been; twenty-two wins in a row and then, suddenly, down – but only for a short time. They had another great run but it was too late; Barça had closed the gap and the damage was done.

They got *too* good and they didn't know where to go

next – you can see that the group is still suffering from that – and I don't think that's because of the manager; it's because of the players. Sometimes you get to a point where you wonder, 'How can I get them stimulated again?' Sometimes it just doesn't work out.

Obviously, when you make a decision it could be right or wrong. You cannot look back at the end of the season and say, 'Oh, I should have done this, I should have done that,' that's very easy. He's always been, or at least he gives me the impression that he's always been, consistent and original with his decisions. When you look at his results over all the teams he's managed across many countries, you have to say that the way he manages is the right way for him, because he has been so successful.

When I look at Carlo I see a real gentleman – he's super-respectful and he doesn't pretend to be someone that he's not, which in the modern game is difficult. Add to that the fact that he clearly has a winning formula. Whatever he does, he gets teams working together, playing together and winning together. Trust me, Paris Saint-Germain is as difficult a first team as you're going to get and he got them playing in a difficult 4-4-2 formation; he goes to Real Madrid, he gets them winning; he gets to Chelsea, they win the double. It's very easy to say that he's a bit soft or that his management style is wrong, but that's not what the numbers say.

I think that Carlo found his spiritual home at Milan, and to a certain extent he is looking for a similar adventure. He wanted it to be in Paris, but that didn't work out. I don't think it's going to be easy for managers in the future to have a long tenure, not least because they won't be managers, they will be head coaches and they will be more easily removed. Being a head coach is very different from being a manager. As a manager you can plan the next five years, the next ten years – build the club, play young players – and you can get stimulation and enjoyment from seeing it develop. That's a long-term ambition. It seems to me that Carlo could have stayed at any of his clubs for much longer and he would have had as much long-term success as he did at Milan.

Just as a player needs to find their highest level, so a manager needs to have constant stimulation. You wouldn't last more than three years unless there was something else to achieve, and sometimes as a manager, if you haven't got a link with a football club, it's very difficult to build one. It's very rare what Arsène Wenger has done at Arsenal. He's constantly finding means of stimulation: building a new stadium, winning the Premier League, winning the FA Cup, getting into the Champions League, constantly creating his own challenges.

As a head coach you're always only thirty minutes away from losing your job – there's no more security. As a manager, however, you can have a five-year, a ten-year plan. When I was with Dave Whelan at Wigan, the last thing he would be worried about each weekend was the result, because he had a long-term philosophy. It's the same with my chairman now at Everton, Bill Kenwright. We're looking at Ross Barkley, John Stones, Brendan Galloway – players of nineteen, twenty, twenty-one years old – and we're looking at them to hit full potential. It's long term – that only happens with managers. You cannot do that sort of strategy with a head coach. When Carlo went to Madrid, he had to beat Barcelona or he had to win the Champions League – or even better, both. That's a short-term strategy.

Carlo knew he was one goal away from the sack because if they don't win the Champions League, he's gone, in one season. Some managers lost their job after winning their domestic league – Fabio Capello, Vicente del Bosque. That's how impossible longevity is in a job like that. That's why Carlo's relationships at Milan were so important. He was there as a player – he's an icon there.

In fact, Carlo can look at any player and say, 'Look, I used to do that ten times better than you,' and there's no way back for the player. People in England don't remember what a great player he was. He was a central part of that glorious Milan team with the Dutch players, which was the best for three or four seasons.

In the top leagues in Europe, the only way of working for the long term is with a manager, and clubs like Chelsea don't have that role; they've got a director of football and other people upstairs assembling the squad. I think you need to be in control of building the squad and working with finances and planning things and have some sort of vision and strategy in order to have a long-term future with a club. It's chicken and egg. Carlo is one of the few to have had both a long-term job, at Milan, and the more modern two- to three-year tenures on his CV. He may well be unique.

PART THREE
Learning to Lead

CHRIS BRADY

Leaders do not emerge fully formed from the womb with all the skills needed to take on the world. Every experience along the road to their eventual success, or failure, adds to the person the world sees when the mantle of leadership is assumed. Key learning experiences begin early, and for all of us these experiences are predominantly 'informal', in that they do not occur in a traditional educational setting. For someone immersed in the bubble of world football, it is especially relevant. Unlike in North America, where sporting development tends to take place in the universities, international football brings children into the bubble at a very early age and formal education is not the highest priority in the minds of the clubs. For them, it is about grooming a future asset.

As such, when the player comes to the end of his playing career, his education as a potential manager has been almost entirely experiential, which need not be a bad thing. Management educator Henry Mintzberg has argued that experiential learning followed by traditional learning is actually the best trajectory; unfortunately, we have created an educational system that is the reverse of this.

At the world's current number one business school, INSEAD, they have a Learning to Lead programme which identifies that:

the transition from being a great individual contributor to being a leader of others is one of the most important and challenging career stages. The Learning to Lead programme is designed to help participants understand the nature of this transition, develop critical people skills and equip them with a whole new skillset that will lead to a smoother transition and, ultimately, career success. (http://executive-education.insead.edu/learning_to_lead)

Footballers rarely, if ever, get the opportunity to engage with such high-powered programmes and instead have to rely on their own personal learning skills.

Experiential learning tends to be described in one of two ways: first, as learning achieved as a result of applying knowledge, intuition and skills in a task-directed setting; second, as learning that occurs as a consequence of simply encountering life, with participants reflecting on the activities in which they engage and internalizing that reflection.

Football managers only have the latter to fall back on. As Dr Steve Kempster of Lancaster University has argued, leaders without any formal leadership training must become informal learners themselves; they must actually address leadership as a phenomenon to be studied in its own right. That way, he argues, they 'will begin to see it everywhere, on television, [in] films, with customers and suppliers, fellow directors and managers and many of the employees'. As a consequence, they will develop the style of leadership that is distinctively their own. This is crucial to the authenticity that is commonly held to be essential to great leadership. 'To thine own self be true' may sound clichéd, but if you are not, you will surely be found out.

The research into this type of learning tends to define it as 'situated learning' – what is more commonly known as learning on the job. Apprenticeships, currently seeing a resurgence in popularity, are another form of situated learning. The key elements of this type of learning are seen as being:

the expert knowledge and skill that can be gained from everyday experiences at work and in the community or family; domain-specific knowledge is necessary for the development of expertise (i.e. much of expertise relies on detailed local knowledge of a workplace, locality or industry); learning is a social process; and, knowledge is embedded in practice and transformed through goal-directed behaviour. (M. Tennant, *Psychology and Adult Learning*, 2nd edn, Routledge, 1999)

Warren Bennis, in his book *Learning to Lead* (Basic Books, 2010), has argued that the old command-and-control approach is no longer appropriate to modern business. Modern businesses, he contends, need skills of orchestration, counselling, collaboration through self-examination, introspection, soul-searching, learning from failure and the cultivation of innate gifts. While all this may be true, in moments of crisis, command-and-control is precisely the leadership style required – and football management is a continual crisis-management profession. Like many theses on leadership, Bennis misses the point of the necessity of being able to employ a range of leadership techniques appropriate to the demands of the business and the owners. Carlo Ancelotti has that ability, and it has been learned in an entirely experiential and situated way. He is the archetypal informal learner and the epitome of what can be achieved under these conditions. It is a common misperception that footballers are not intelligent. Nothing could be further from the truth:

footballers may rarely be educated, but that does not preclude high levels of intelligence.

Another increasingly common topic in leadership literature is the necessity for leaders to learn to 'switch off' and be able to walk away from the continual crises in their work. Most leaders will tell you how difficult this is, but it is one of Carlo's greatest strengths.

A recent survey by the Institute of Leadership and Management revealed that stress over mounting workload meant that one in eight (13 per cent) people in leadership roles question whether holidays are actually 'worth it'. Over half of managers work while on annual leave; seven in ten feel more stressed in the run-up to a holiday; and almost a fifth return from holiday more stressed than when they left.

The report goes on to argue that we take annual leave with the intention of relaxing, unwinding and recharging the batteries, but holidays aren't as relaxing as we would hope them to be. Over half of all employees feel compelled to work while on annual leave. Worries over mounting workload were revealed as the biggest barrier to rest and relaxation. With technology making us contactable anytime and anywhere, an overwhelming 80 per cent of managers reported that they check their BlackBerry or smartphone on holiday.

This is not good business and there are good reasons why it is essential to take time off:

- No one is indispensable.
- Getting away enables reflection that can identify gaps in your management structure and operations.
- It gives others the opportunity to step up.
- Regular breaks allow leaders to recharge, rest, pursue other interests and come back energized.
- It prevents burn-out and illness.

Carlo Ancelotti intrinsically understands the importance of switching off (see Chapter 10). For example before starting at Bayern Munich in July 2016, he will spend time at home in Vancouver – cooking, reading, spending time with family. But simultaneously he was watching games from around the world, talking to key contacts – quietly learning, quietly influencing.

Carlo doesn't divide his time into 'work' and 'holiday' modes, or indeed divide his own self-perception into 'manager' or 'family man'. On the contrary, he is always fully engaged in both football and the world. As Jean Lave and Etienne Wenger put it, learning to lead 'involves the whole person; it implies not only a relation to specific activities, but a relation to social communities – it implies becoming a full participant, a member, a kind of person'.*

In this section, Carlo will look at how, from his humble beginnings in rural Italy, he learned to become the leader that he is today.

*J. Lave and E. Wenger, *Situated Learning: Legitimate Peripheral Participation* (Cambridge University Press, 1991), p. 53.

9. Growing

The Seeds of Leadership

I was born into a very poor family – my father, mother, sister, grandfather and grandmother, all living together in the same house. My father was a farmer and he and my grandfather worked on the land. My father worked very hard. Every day he started at four in the morning and worked until six, seven or even eight o'clock at night. I learned a lot about discipline and the importance of a strong work ethic – he was a good reference, my father.

We had ten cows to make milk and Parmesan cheese. This was the only work in the area – there was no real industry, just farming. We'd earn money from the cheese and a little from making wine. We had a small vineyard for the wine, but mostly this was for our own consumption. We would sell the excess, which was not a lot. The most important part was the cheese. The problem was that it took a year before it was ready to sell and we could get some money for it, so my father needed to control our finances very carefully each year, waiting for the payment. You know when you are rich because you don't know exactly how much is in your bank account; my father knew to the exact penny what we had. We needed to be organized.

This time was to be my first lesson on the importance of the owner. When I was very young my father was working the land but didn't own the property. In Italy at the time you could work on the property of one owner, but 50 per cent of what you made went to that owner. At the beginning I was upset because I didn't understand. We would work hard in the fields and have a huge pile of grain in the front of the house, but then the owner would arrive with a piece of wood and put it down the middle of the pile and say, 'This is mine.' It was the same with the chickens. I hated this person, but they were the rules. I never saw my father angry with these people. I only saw my father happy – never nervous, never aggressive. It was a happy period for me. We didn't have money, but I remember this time as a really happy period in my life, with plenty of laughter. When you don't have anything, you don't know how poor you are. But I did begin to realize then that it was important to have money, like the landowner.

When I first went to play for Roma I went directly to the president to try to agree a contract – at that time there were no agents. I was twenty years old, had come from a team in the third division, and I asked for 100 million lire a year. He said to me, 'You are totally crazy.'

At that time a good job could earn maybe 10 million lire.

Of course, without a contract I couldn't play, so the president said to me, 'Listen, it's not so important what are you earning. It's more important what are you saving.'

'I can save a lot more with 100 million,' I said.

We remained at an impasse until the last day I could sign and be able to play. The president finally offered me 20 million and I accepted. I had only asked for such an amount because my friend, an older guy, who I thought must know what he's talking about, had said that the club paid a lot of money to sign me, so I should ask for 100 million. No wonder the president thought I was crazy. You should always know what you're talking about before you start a negotiation.

When I signed for the academy at Parma, which was far from my family home, I tried to travel home every day after school and after training, but it was exhausting. I left my family the next year, at the age of fifteen, to go to a college in Parma close to the training ground. Because it was a religious college, for priests, I lived there but I went to a normal school outside. Living in the college was really tough, but it was a great experience for me. Away from my family for the first time, I learned that I had to organize my day by myself. I had to be self-disciplined: go to school then to training, study, clean my own clothes. It was hard in the beginning. I also learned what bad food was like. With my family the food had always been special.

When planning my day, I had to fit in prayers at the church, in the morning and before I went to bed. Everything was regimented at the college. When I went to training I still had to get a card to sign in and out, even though they knew that I was playing for Parma. There was no flexibility.

Of course, my mother had not wanted me to leave home, which was why I had commuted in the first year at Parma. Eventually, though, she saw how tired I was with the travelling and how it was affecting my training. She knew that I dreamed to go – I wanted to play football.

I would go home at the weekend, after school on the Saturday, and usually we played on Sunday morning. My father would usually take me to play – sometimes my uncle – and I would come back home and stay until Monday morning, when I would travel back to school. I found it really difficult and I was very sad.

Being away was a hard experience to adapt to for me because I was born in a little village where everyone knew each other. I had a lot of friends in my small village but I'd never been on holiday or away before – I didn't go to the beach until I was fifteen years old. My holiday was to stay on the farm, in my house and maybe go to Parma. At that time, going to Parma was like going from London to Vancouver today. It took the whole day.

Gradually, I learned to adapt and make friends. The four years in the college helped me overcome my shyness and timidity. Aside from two or three of us, most of the people staying there were not players, just schoolboys. They were guys who had come from outside Parma and who couldn't go to their local schools for some reason or another. They were all from a similar background to me – farms and small villages.

I didn't really learn about other regions or nationalities until I started to play for Nils Liedholm, my Swedish manager at Roma. He was the first person I'd met who was from another country. I thought all Swedes were like him but, after Liedholm, I had another Swede manage me at Roma, Sven-Göran Eriksson, and I soon learned that Liedholm was Liedholm, not a Swede. It was from him that I learned that it was possible to be flexible. There were no rules so strict that they had to be obeyed at all times. We could have training scheduled for eleven o'clock, but it wouldn't start until eleven fifteen because he was late. Sometimes we would ask him why and he would always answer, 'Because I'm working for you. I was busy doing things to make your life easier.' I was never late but it was OK for him to be late. When we had lunch or dinner, everyone could choose what they wanted – there was always some flexibility. When you make a decision, you take into consideration the thoughts of the people involved, to understand what they are thinking. Liedholm did this. He was very smart.

Teammates

When I started to play in the professional team at Parma my first leaders were the older players who gave me orders. I was the kid and I would have to carry their bags everywhere, sometimes clean their boots as part of my apprenticeship. I didn't know if it was fair or not. It was an unspoken rule that the youngest just did as they were told, so I didn't argue. I also heard the young players at Manchester United used to have to clean the boots for the first-team players. The famous Class of '92 – Paul Scholes, Ryan Giggs, David Beckham and the rest – said they did this under Sir Alex when they were young, but I don't think this happens any more.

I wasn't happy to take the loudest person who gave the most orders as the leader. I looked around for the real leader, the most important player in the team. I knew it would be the player who had more personality and influence, who was a real professional and an example to the rest. At Parma this player was Lucio Mongardi.

At that time Parma were in the third division and Mongardi was one of only a few players in the team to have played in Serie A, with his previous club, Atalanta. He took care of me because I was younger and he saw the qualities in me to be a professional. Sometimes he invited me to his house to have lunch or dinner with his family. He was my reference as a man and he was also my reference as a player, because he was the playmaker in the team, the position I wanted to play.

I realized that this was the way to lead. I knew that to just give orders did not feel correct. It was not fair, because I wanted to be treated like the others. I was young, OK, but I was a player like everyone else. If I was not worth as much as the others then why was I in the team? Maybe I did not earn as much as the others, but if I played in the team then surely I should be treated as an equal. Mongardi was the only one who thought that way. Everyone in the team should be equal.

Mongardi was not an arrogant player. He didn't use his power to bully the young players, and this was an important lesson for me. Maybe he was also empathetic because he had been in Serie A and come back down. He'd done it all and didn't have anything to prove, so his ego was in the right place.

He was the leader of the team but he was not the captain. As was traditional in Italy at the time, the captain was the player who had spent the most years at the club. I saw this, that the captain was just a senior player, and could equally see that Mongardi was what I now call the technical leader. He had the experience in Serie A, the most knowledge on the pitch, and he was a great example to the rest of the team. I followed his behaviour and, when my chance came to play in Serie A with Roma, I knew what would be expected of me there thanks to him.

Managers

When I arrived at Roma I didn't need to look for the leader among the players because the leader was the manager. Agostino Di Bartolomei was the captain, born in Rome and from the Roma academy, but only appeared to be the leader to those outside the squad. He was, perhaps, the political leader. He had a strong relationship with the press, the supporters and the club, and maybe the manager saw him as a leader, but among the players he was not viewed in the same way. He was effective in his role, but inside the dressing room he was one of us.

For me, it was the manager, Nils Liedholm, who led the squad, which was unusual. He was quiet but strong. When I became a manager myself later, I met him and it was a little bit uncomfortable. He was still my father. In Russian they say the boss is not always right but he is always the boss, and this is the way it was for me with Liedholm.

Because of his natural authority he would not even answer if you challenged him; he would simply pose a question back to you and you would know what he wanted you to do. At the end of my first season at the club I decided to rent an apartment with a friend in the squad and move out of our accommodation at the training ground. We went to see Liedholm in his office and explained our plan.

'Are you sure?' he asked. 'Yes,' we said, 'we are sure.' 'OK, no problem for me,' he said, 'but I think that you both need to train with the academy, not with the first team. If you want to train with the first team, you have to stay, to live at the training ground.' We looked at each other and said, together, 'OK, we'll stay at the training ground.'

Sometimes in a squad, players get unhappy and complain about the manager, but no one spoke badly about Liedholm. Everyone had complete respect for him. When the Brazilian player Falcao arrived, Liedholm gave him his blessing and the power to lead.

Falcao was a player with great professional quality. You

know immediately when you see a leader – it's the personality, the character. It's not the technical skills. Falcao was one of the first foreign players I had come across and it was like he was from another planet. He was not used to our style of training, so he had to adjust. In Brazil they trained with the ball a lot, while in Italy, at that time, not so much.

Liedholm slowly began to alter our training sessions, not only to help Falcao, but also because he was learning from the player. We began to have more sessions with the ball and fewer without it. Liedholm changed our training a little and Falcao a little, so we could meet closer to the middle. When a squad contains players from several different cultures, the top managers take the best from each. What Falcao brought was an attitude of, 'Why is the ball not here? Why are we not training with the ball more?'

Communication is key here – it is the basis of every relationship. What you say, how you say it and when you say it. Everybody has their own character and their own style of communication. There are players who need to be stimulated and there are those who prefer to delegate, while other players are foot soldiers who just want to execute orders. A manager has to take into consideration all these differences in personality and must listen to what each player thinks, because for players to give their all they have to be convinced about what they are doing. The manager has to be willing to listen and change his ideas if it means the chance of greater success. It is a lesson I fully embraced later in my career when I did things like change Andrea Pirlo's

position in the team and talk to Sergio Ramos about playing in midfield.

Liedholm had such confidence in his own power that he
gave the players a lot of responsibility. He was not strict in
his tactics. He would give us some information, not a lot,
and the players had freedom on the pitch, which, of course,
created a better relationship with the manager. In this way
he was creating new leaders. Falcao became a coach, I am a
coach and Liedholm was our guide.

He was never afraid to delegate, whether on the pitch to
the players or off the pitch to the trainers for the physical
preparation. Although he loved to be on the pitch he inter-
fered only very rarely, if he saw something badly wrong. Even
then it would not be with anger, but with care. It was a different style of training compared with today and he really
loved to be on the pitch to teach the players about technical
rather than tactical aspects. He loved to fine-tune the players, and with top players this is all that is necessary. He
could stay for two hours just working on a technical
exercise.

He was always professional even when he was joking,
which couldn't always be said of the players, but that is how
it was in those days. Now I can say that the players are more
professional – they can sometimes see it as a job. When I
started we just thought it was great to play *and* get paid. Life
was good. It is important to remember this because, even
today, ultimately the players just want to play.

The big change today is a player's status. Now they make

their own choices, but when I played we were the property of the club. We didn't know from year to year what was going to happen to us because it was not our decision – we were owned. I didn't know if I would be able to earn more money in the next year or if I would leave the club. Now the players take more care of themselves and are closer to being masters of their own destiny. Because the situation regarding contracts and salaries is now so different from in the past, I have to recognize that players should be treated as individuals with a personal agenda.

Would a manager like Liedholm manage successfully in today's game? Yes, of course. He would adapt. He would understand that this new professionalism is more intense, that there is less opportunity for fun. On the training ground the players always work hard because it is their profession. For me, professionalism is linked to the intensity that you use when you train – physical intensity, but above all mental intensity. This is what the modern manager must deal with at all times when the players are working.

Of course, today there are very different off-field pressures on both the players and the coaches. As a manager I cannot control the player when he is away from the club. All I can do is give information about the type of behaviour I expect, which is to eat sensibly, drink responsibly and get enough sleep – to live a normal life and be able to integrate with others. Everyone is entitled to a private life away from the club, but if a player does these things and works hard at his job, then I am happy with him.

It was while I was at Roma that I was first asked to be a leader. Sven-Göran Eriksson had taken over from Liedholm and Agostino Di Bartolomei had left the club, so Eriksson asked me to be captain. I thought, 'All I have to do is take the armband, talk to the referee, toss the coin, choose the way to play and talk to the press after the game; does this make me a leader now?' I always thought the captain should set an example for the team, not in what he says, but what he does.

Becoming captain didn't change my idea of professionalism, of the right behaviour, but I did feel more responsibility, of course. It wasn't so much with my immediate teammates – with them nothing changed. I was the same before and after getting the armband. The biggest change for me was with the younger players who came up from the academy. I could be a reference for them in the same way that Mongardi had been for me as a kid at Parma. Just as he had taken care of me, I tried to have conversations with the younger players and to take care of them as well. I remembered what had happened to me as a kid and I didn't want our younger players to have the same bad experiences. I tried to give these young players both information and support and, of course, they didn't have to clean the boots.

Even in the short time that I was captain at Roma I started to realize the responsibility that came with being a leader. I began to understand that leading is not about how you see yourself, but how others see you. My responsibility was to be a role model. Every team has its rules, written or unwritten, and the first one who has to respect the rules is the captain. The manager would set the rules, but it was my job to show respect to them. With Liedholm, as I have said, there was flexibility, but with Eriksson it was more strict. Roma was a big club for Eriksson, so maybe he used the rules to bolster his confidence; Liedholm had so much self-confidence that he was able to be more relaxed.

Liedholm's self-belief stemmed not only from having such a great knowledge of the game and his success as a manager, but also from enjoying the status of being one of the best players in the world during his playing career. He used to speak about his playing days in a really funny, self-deprecating way. He played for Milan with two other great Swedish footballers – Gunnar Gren and Gunnar Nordahl – and together they formed the famous Gre-No-Li. He would tell us, 'I didn't misplace a pass in the San Siro for three years and when I finally misplaced one, the whole crowd was so shocked they let out an, "Oooooh!".'

Impossible, we would say, laughing. But he was such a legend among the Milan faithful that they still all tell the same story: At the end of his career, the entire San Siro stadium applauded for five minutes after he misplaced a pass – an acknowledgement of years of infallibility, but mostly an acknowledgement of love.

As relaxed as Liedholm was, there were still issues about which he would be very strict: you have to respect your teammates; you have to respect the manager; you don't fight in the training ground; and you don't speak badly about your teammates. These were his non-negotiable rules.

As must be obvious, I learned a lot from Liedholm. He was, and still is, my most important reference in football.

National Service

I was called up to play for the national team for the first time in a four-team tournament between Uruguay, Italy, Holland and Brazil. In the first game against Holland I scored after seven minutes, which was the second-quickest debut goal in the history of the Italian national team. I played twenty-six matches for the national team and never scored again.

After the game we went back to our hotel to get some rest before the next game against Uruguay in Montevideo, but two of my teammates, Claudio Gentile and Marco Tardelli, said to me, 'Let's go out – we have to celebrate.' I was really nervous about doing this because I was only twenty-one and didn't know if the manager would allow it. Was I allowed to go out after only my first game?

'You have to come,' the players insisted. 'You have to buy a beer for us because you scored the first goal.'

'But what about the manager?'

'Don't worry about the manager – you are with us.'

So, we went out for a beer, nothing crazy. We just talked and drank a few beers, but by the time we returned in a taxi to the hotel it was one in the morning, and who should be stood there, his arms crossed and face like thunder, right in front of the hotel? The manager, of course – the imposing figure of Enzo Bearzot.

'What do we do now?' I said, panicking a little.

'Don't worry, don't worry – we'll go round the back of the hotel.'

We went the back way, through the garage and up to our floor in the lift. The door opened on our floor and there was the manager, waiting for us. 'You and you,' he said to Gentile and Tardelli, 'go to bed.'

'You,' he said to me, 'come with me.' I knew at that moment who would lead and who would follow. Bearzot told me that I had been easily led and he explained to me in no uncertain terms how I should respond in the future. I should always listen, he told me, but I should always make my own decision.

The difference between Bearzot and Liedholm can be seen in another, similar incident. Three of us at Roma pulled up outside our team hotel one night with a couple of girls in the back with us. We saw Liedholm coming out of the hotel and, when he saw us in the car, he came striding over. We had nowhere to go so we just waited for what the English like to call a 'bollocking' from the manager. When he got to the car he motioned to us to roll down the window, which we did, and then he peered inside and very quietly said, 'Is there any room for me?'

That was the difference between Bearzot and Liedholm,

but both were, nonetheless, very successful managers. I could only be like one of them because that is who I am, but I did learn that different styles can be just as effective.

I could not be as rigid as Bearzot was. When I played for him, he always insisted that we play man to man – right up until we played the World Cup in 1986. Man to man, every time. Of course, this approach was perfect for my friend Gentile. The trainers would tell Gentile, 'You have to kick everything that moves on the pitch. Also, the ball. If it's the ball, that's a bonus.' Gentile marked the best players – Zico, Diego Maradona – and he was like a limpet.

I was not used to playing man to man because with Liedholm we were allowed more freedom to defend in zones. In 1984 the national side had a friendly game in Bologna and I was a substitute. When Bearzot eventually called on me to go on, he said, 'Mark number 10.' On the pitch, I tried to see this number 10. I could see number 3, number 14, number 15 – but I didn't find number 10. From the bench, Bearzot was shouting, 'Mark number 10!' Where was he?

The reason I couldn't find number 10 was because he had been substituted without Bearzot noticing. At the end of the game he was angry with me and said, 'I told you to mark number 10!' I tried to explain that he wasn't on the pitch, but you couldn't argue with Bearzot.

Italy won the World Cup in 1982 and we went into the 1986 tournament as strong contenders. It was to be in Mexico, at altitude, 3,000 metres. We went to a mountain in Italy in the middle of winter and, in the morning, we didn't train – we didn't run, we didn't walk – we had a talk instead. There were players asking, 'How can we prepare for a World Cup like this?' But nobody would question the coach. This is not a good environment. We came home from Mexico quickly.

The System

When I left Roma and moved to Milan I was a well-established player, but I was still the new boy. Franco Baresi was the captain but not a natural leader in his personality. He didn't speak much off of the pitch, but on the pitch he was very voluble – talking about the behaviour of the team, about the movement. Sometimes you have it so that the leader has both the technical aspects and personality, but often it comes from different players. One might be a technical leader, another a personality leader.

Milan had been going through some hard times when I joined. The club had a fantastic history in the 1960s and 70s, when they won two European Cups and they had last won the Scudetto in 1979, but the 1980s had not been kind to them. They had been relegated and then promoted again, before Silvio Berlusconi bought the club and invested in the squad.

When I first arrived I was one of the few players to have won something. I had won the Scudetto in 1983, played in the final of the European Cup in 1984 and, at the time,

I was considered to be one of the best midfielders in Italy. This gave me a different status in the group. As a new player I was recognized as a leader because of my history, my achievements and my technical ability. Not for my behaviour, of course, because they did not know my behaviour yet. I became a reference for some of the other players.

Your past achievements always help you when you arrive at a new place. It makes it easier for you to be respected. When I arrived at Madrid as a manager I had won two Champions Leagues and the players immediately had a lot of respect for me. After that, they are going to judge you, but at the beginning you have an advantage. You have to use this period to build a relationship with the players. Don't show an ego, don't brag. Sure, I could show an ego, brag about what I'd won, but I'd lose the respect of the players immediately. When I arrived in Milan as a player I was respected for my past and, just like I would come to know as a manager, you have a honeymoon period until the first training session and then the players begin to judge you.

Milan had three excellent Dutch players: Frank Rijkaard, a physical, talented player; Marco van Basten, a fantastic technical player; and Ruud Gullit, a complete footballer and strong character. Ruud was one of the leaders, always trying to motivate and light a fire under someone if necessary. It was the foreign players who seemed to have the strongest personalities in that team.

However, despite all the strong characters and my own position in the group, it was the system that led the ·

team – always the system that had to be observed. This was manager Arrigo Sacchi's way. The three players who became the references were me, Baresi and Gullit, but only because we served the system. Sacchi's tactics were different from everybody else's at the time. He wanted quick penetration, so Baresi had to press a high line from the back, Gullit, one of the best forwards in the world, was required to work really hard and my job was to link the defence and attack, moving the ball quickly. Some modern coaches are similar to Sacchi like this – press high, win the ball back in forward positions and then strike quickly. Speed is first, possession second.

Sacchi's path to becoming the coach of Milan was unusual. He was not a famous player. His father had a shoe company and he went to work for it, selling footwear in Holland during the 1970s. At that time, Ajax had developed the concept of Total Football, in which players can change positions and play attack and defence, all together. Sacchi was fascinated by this and studied it at every opportunity. He then returned to Italy and worked his way up through the divisions, until he arrived at Milan. He came to us with what were fresh ideas about football.

Because Gullit, Baresi and I were the keys to implementing his ideas, we were his representatives on the pitch, so to speak. Sacchi had signed me – despite the doubts about my fitness expressed by Galliani and Berlusconi – to be the centre of the team. He believed that I had the footballing intelligence to understand what was needed to make his ideas work.

When Sacchi bought a player, he did a lot of research not just on their technical skills, but on their personality – their private life and behaviour. He told me that he sent his friend to watch our training sessions for fifteen days so he could get an idea of my attitude on the training pitch. He wanted to be sure that I was professional. He knew what he wanted and how hard we would have to work in order to achieve it, but he also knew that with everything in place we could beat all the teams in Serie A.

Despite having had some problems with my knees, I still had to work harder at Milan than when I was a player for Roma – harder than I had ever worked before. The job Sacchi wanted from me was to move backwards and forwards a lot, to support both Baresi and Gullit, respectively. To ensure that we knew the exact distance we needed to be from each other, Sacchi would sometimes tie us together with a rope. At the beginning we thought he was crazy. I lost six kilograms in weight in those first three seasons with Sacchi. When I arrived home to see my family one day, my mother answered the door and said, 'Who are you? They are trying to kill my son!'

GROWING: THE QUIET WAY

- Rules can be elastic but, like a balloon, there are limits. Let everyone know what your limits are.
- Self-confidence breeds confidence. In the words of Mike, the conman in David Mamet's *House of Games*, 'Why do they call it a confidence trick? Because you give me your confidence? No, because I give you mine.' Great leaders give confidence.
- It can be difficult to see yourself as the leader. Remember, if someone has given you the job they believe in you, so trust their judgement.
- In general, people love the job they're in. Don't kill that love.
- Intensity is good. But remember, you don't have to be miserable to be serious.

IN THEIR OWN WORDS . . . THE PLAYERS

PAOLO MALDINI ON CARLO

Carletto remains what he has always been with me. He manages to crack jokes even before the final of the Champions League. We were a family at Milan and that's what families do. For Carlo the idea of family is everything; it all comes back to that. He never gets angry – well, *almost* never. I'm sure every player has maybe one story to tell about him going crazy in the dressing room.

Out of all the leadership techniques I've witnessed, his is definitely the least problematic. He holds in all his own worries and pressures and so the team preserves its tranquillity. From time to time, though, even the most patient man in the world loses his cool.

My favourite story was when he exploded in Lugano, after a preseason exhibition game against the Swiss team. He looked like he'd lost his mind. He said the worst things to us, peppering us with insults – horrible, unforgivable things that I couldn't possibly repeat to you. He just kept it up and I suddenly felt like laughing. He'd gone completely off the rails and I'd never seen him like that before. He turned beet red, and sitting next to him was Adriano Galliani, wearing a bright yellow tie. Together, they looked like a rainbow.

Two days later he came to us and asked for our forgiveness. He could never be mean through and through. He's a teddy bear, deep down. The secret of our track record is the fact that he's a regular guy. There's no need for him to be the Special One to win. It's enough to have an inner tranquillity and to stay out of the limelight, to keep from setting off fireworks in front of the television cameras.

Carletto and I have always had a comfortable and close working relationship. We've always talked about everything. Whenever he loses his temper, he unfailingly comes to me afterwards and asks: 'Paolo, was I wrong?' Carlo doesn't want to do everything on his own, he wants to bring people with him and delegate, which is a sign of his considerable intelligence. This is why he can win wherever he goes: at AC Milan, at Chelsea, at Real Madrid – anywhere. His knowledge of global football is enormous. He has mind-boggling experience of every aspect of the game. Even as a player he was an outstanding organizer and reader of the game, full of ideas. You can't really criticize him, in either technical or human terms: if you do, you're not being fair.

At AC Milan, from the times of Arrigo Sacchi onwards, we've had lots of coaches, nearly all of them winners, but each has managed the group in his own manner. Leaving aside the question of methods and results, if I were asked who brought the highest quality of life in those years, I'd have to say it was Carletto. Before he came to Milanello, he was fairly rigid, less open to tactical innovation, but over time he grew. He evolved, and we evolved with him, because you need to give a man like that players who know enough not to take advantage of him. Underlying everything that we did was a two-way trust. Over the years there have been people who took advantage of the situation, but we were quick to make sure they understood how to behave. In particular, we explained to them that they had to respect Carletto, always, and no matter what, because of the magical football he seems to be able to conjure up, for the way he talks to his team and for the way he behaves off the field.

Everybody in this book will describe him in a thousand different ways. For me, he is a friend and I miss him.

10. Values

Managing the Madness

People outside the game sometimes wonder how I go about 'managing the madness' that is football today. For me, it's normal. It's all I have known since I left home some forty years ago. I was a player for nearly twenty years and now a coach for even longer. I only know this madness.

Of course, I see the statistics. In England the job with the highest turnover is chambermaid and the second is football coach. The League Managers Association send me their magazine every month and I'm shocked and saddened when I see that if the manager of an English club lasts more than twenty-seven months he is defined as 'long term'. In Italy, the period would be more like twenty-seven hours.

I also see that less than half of football coaches in England ever get another job in football if they are sacked from their first post. They never come back into the game. I recall how close I was to getting the sack in my first job at Reggiana – after seven games, when we were bottom of the table. The only thing that saved me was my name. I was still famous for being a player and I was from the region. Today, I feel so lucky – so privileged and thankful – to be at the top of this profession, because I know that it could easily have been so different.

People say that the madness is because of the fans, but I cannot control that. In my job there are three things that I cannot control: the president, the supporters and the media. I have learned not to worry so much about these. What would be the point? I want to work on what I can control, and that is my relationship with the players. That is my only job. Admittedly, they can be mad too, but at least I am limiting the chaos.

Madness or not, I love my job. I respect the people that I work with and I have the respect from those that work with me. It's the perfect role. If I can't be a player any more, then this is what I want. They say that if you are in a job you love, you never work a day in your life, and it's true.

I get so much out of working with the elite performers in the game. By that I mean the people who display the three different components of the top players: first, their own individual talent; second, the contextual talent – how they fit in, culturally; and third, their team talent – how much they contribute. The talent is not complete if a player only uses it for himself. To be a great champion, a truly great player, it's not enough just to have individual talent. Everyone might know that you are very talented, but to be *fuoriclasse*, as we say in Italy – out of the ordinary, a cut above – you must have it all. To watch this flourish as part of a team I'm managing – it's fantastic.

References

I hope I have made it clear throughout this book just how important it is to have people as 'reference points' – people who set an example and act as role models by doing the right things. For me, when I was very young, I looked up to Sandro Mazzola – after my father, of course. I was an Inter fan in those days and he was my favourite player because I thought he was the strongest. He could be a striker or offensive midfielder and I loved the technique of his play.

My favourite quotation about teamwork is from basketball's Michael Jordan, perhaps one of the greatest ever individual players in world sport, but an even greater team player. It is a quotation that should be on every dressing-room wall:

> There are plenty of teams, in every sport, that have great players and never win titles. Most of the time, those players aren't willing to sacrifice for the greater good of the team. The funny thing is, in the end, their unwillingness to sacrifice only makes individual goals more difficult to achieve. One thing I believe to the fullest is that if you think and achieve as a team, the individual accolades will take care of themselves. Talent wins games but teamwork and intelligence win championships.

I love the movies and I have always been a fan of Robert De Niro. Nowhere does he embody all the ideals I hold about him more than in *The Deer Hunter.* I've seen this movie maybe ten times and the main thing for me is that it's all about friendship and relying on each other in the most extreme situations.

It is the same with another favourite of mine at the moment, *Life Is Beautiful.* Again, the situation is terrible but the solution is great. What I like is the idea that one man is able to change a bad situation through irony while remaining within it. He makes the situation bearable for his son while dealing with the reality himself. This is sacrifice.

I love *The Godfather.* The film shows that the two most important things are respect and calm authority. Vito Corleone is a leader who should be a reference because he was respected by everyone – the family, friends, the people who worked with him and even his enemies. Of course, I know that he does bad things and that the Mafia is a criminal organization, but what I am talking about is the way his family operated internally, the respect. I know some would say that it is fear and not respect, but it is fear born of a recognition that he is the leader. They are the same qualities, albeit in a bad direction, as those who lead for good.

I am impressed by people who work to find new ideas, no matter what their field is. After visiting a cardiology convention in San Francisco, I invested in a company that is developing a new valve to help people with heart problems. It's unbelievable, what it can do. I have a friend who wants to do movie animation. The sheer amount of work they have to put in, painting thousands of images to create it, impresses me. I'm interested in how people are able to think differently. In football we do not do this enough – and I include myself in this. We need to think more laterally.

Switching Off

I have to admit to being a little obsessive, but this is true of most successful people – especially professional ath-letes. How else can you explain the hours and hours of repetitive practice needed to be of the required technical standard, and that's before the hours needed to understand the game, to manage the game. I am obsessive about order. Everything for me is tidy and organized. Even things like my clothes – I know exactly where my white shirts are, my blue shirts. The little details – they are all in order. I get this from being with the priests, when I lived at the college at Parma. I had a tiny room, so I had to be organized.

I am still obsessive and it is still all about the game. For me, money is not so important as long as I have enough not to worry. Zlatan and I would often sit and talk about how we got to where we are. We are both from poor backgrounds and find it difficult to believe we are wealthy enough not to worry. When I read that some managers insist on being the highest paid at the club – higher even than all the players – I am surprised.

I've never insisted on that. I've accepted that as a manager you can always find a player who earns more than you, because . . . let's face it, the players *are* more important than you. Which person in football thinks that the manager is more important than the players? There is not one. The supporters think that the players are the most important, the president thinks the same, and the players – they certainly know that they are the most important. The only time the manager is the most important for everyone is when the team is losing. The manager is only important when there needs to be someone to blame.

People have said to me, 'Why would you pay a player more than you earn?' For me, money is not the key driver; success drives me. So it's simple. If I am to be successful then I need the best players, and if the best players cost more than I do, I want them playing for me. I'm actually being selfish, really, not nice.

The president of Roma back when I was playing, Dino Viola, said to me, 'It's not important what you earn, it's important what you save; but remember, the more you earn, the more you will be respected.' This last bit he added only after he'd negotiated my first contract with me, of course.

With all the demands on my time – to deal with the players, the game, the people at the club, the media, the latest developments and the opposition – and the pressures in the game – to get results, play attractive football and keep my job – there is a lot, you might imagine, to keep me up at night. Earlier in my career it was true: I would stay awake agonizing over decisions – that's my obsessive nature again. But now I'm able to switch off well.

Experience helps, of course, and it's important to have a happy home to go back to. My home life is my sanctuary, where I recharge my batteries, and this is crucial when things are not going well, such as after a bad result or even losing my job. I like to lose myself in the domestic environment. I love to cook at home. You may have noticed the importance I attach to mealtime, as a social thing, for people to bond. Maybe that's being Italian.

Football, however, is my life, my passion, my hobby, and I never really 'leave' football. As the Eagles say about Hotel California, you might be able to check out, but leaving isn't an option. Switching off is my checkout time from football, but I'll never leave.

The only time I have any difficulty sleeping is when we lose a game, because then I start replaying every part of the game in my mind. I work out what we must do to improve, what I have to tell the players the day after.

During weeks when there are no matches I have no problem at all sleeping. I like the Spanish approach, to have a short sleep after lunch – just an hour or two – when we have a game in the evening. Some of the players also sleep then, and we are only beginning to understand now just important sleep is for recovery, for strength, for the brain. We need to know more about it. Luckily for me, I'm good at it.

VALUES: THE QUIET WAY

- Always keep your reference points in mind – from early mentors to those whose achievements you aspire to follow.
- Switching off is important – find your sanctuary.
- To thine own self be true – you can't actually be anyone else, so don't try.

IN THEIR OWN WORDS . . . THE PLAYERS

ALESSANDRO NESTA ON CARLO

I first met Carlo five months before I signed for Milan because I was with the national team, training at Milanello. He was around the training ground a lot and he came to me and said, 'Next season, you have to come here.' 'No, no, no,' I said. 'I don't like here. I want to stay at Lazio because you know I am a Lazio fan. Also, I don't like Milan; I prefer Rome.' Three months later I signed for Milan.

Carlo was the most important coach in my career because he changed my mentality. In Rome it was different: playing for Lazio meant that, if you won the derby against Roma, it's a good season. In Milan, you have to win every single game – if not, next season you will be out. He taught me that, at a club like Milan, every game is like a cup final. Carlo played for Milan and coached Milan – he knew the Milan way. He explained that this was the culture of the club, and if I wanted to stay at Milan for a long time I needed to learn it early and maintain that standard every day, in every training session. If not, goodbye Sandro.

In training Carlo was very strong. He would build a winning mentality throughout the club. This is the difference between a club like Manchester City and Manchester United. Manchester United has a big history with a culture of winning. When you sign for Manchester United, nothing is acceptable except winning. Manchester City are building, but they don't have a history. Milan has that history.

I took a while to settle after leaving Rome – I wasn't happy at first. Carlo helped me by constantly reminding me of the professionalism I had to show each and every day. 'Remember,' he told me, 'this is the best place for you to be. If you want to be the best then you have to follow the best. Watch and learn from Maldini, from Alessandro Costacurta – from all the Milan professionals. If you follow them, you will understand what to do.' If I behaved like that, then I could stay for ever.

I became a better player at Milan. Before, I had played like I was alone among the other defenders, playing for myself, but at Milan we practised three or four times a week with five defenders – Maldini, Cafu, Costacurta, Kakha Kaladze and me – plus the goalkeeper and central defensive midfielder. This was when Andrea Pirlo was learning his new role.

When I think about Carlo, I naturally compare him with other coaches I have played for, like Dino Zoff and Sven-Göran

Eriksson. Eriksson was a good coach and a good person, but if you ask me what the difference was, I won two Champions Leagues with Carlo. We worked together for maybe eight years but it was different, because Carlo had to have extra skills to coach at Milan. It's a difficult club because you have Silvio Berlusconi and Adriano Galliani and they push you and press you every day. Galliani is strong but Berlusconi is worse, trust me. But Carlo made sure that no problems ever found their way to the team. He was a wall between the team and those two, which is very important, especially when they tried to put pressure on the players. It's vital to have a coach like Carlo in these situations. He's the best.

When you talk about Carlo and the game you have to understand how clever he is with his tactics, He was always prepared to listen and learn and then to change if he thought it would benefit the team. He thinks about the game and he's not afraid to change.

At Milan he switched a lot tactically. When I arrived Pirlo was a number 10, an attacking midfielder, but Carlo understood that the right position for him was in front of the back line. The team changed because with Pirlo there the others had to be aware that they could get into better positions. Andriy Shevchenko was more able to play on the edge of the opposition's back line and know that Pirlo could deliver the pass for him to go behind. Carlo recognized this and convinced Pirlo to play there.

Carlo was always very clear about identifying mistakes. 'This is your mistake – look at the video,' he'd say. For me that's no problem. Carlo's relationship with the senior players meant that he could address the players about anything, and they had so much respect for him that they would accept and own up to their mistakes.

Carlo knows that, if you have a champion, a top player, you can say where they went wrong and they will not be upset – they will learn from it. When you go down to the second division, third division, the players are different. They are more defensive because they are less confident. But when you work with, say, Cristiano Ronaldo, you can say anything, because a champion is a champion and they understand. Carlo was a champion as a player and as a coach, so he knows this. I listened and learned from the best.

For the great players, winning is everything, and as long as the coach can help you win, you listen. I know everyone likes to talk about when we lost to Liverpool in the Champions League final in 2005, so I will talk about it – but you must understand that I prefer to speak about when we win. When we won Carlo always said he was 100 per cent sure we were going to win – he was very confident. But when we lost, such as in that final, people ask if it was Carlo's fault. Whose fault was it? I say it was our fault, the players, because when we got to half-time we had played the best half ever. In the dressing room, he said, 'Come on, guys, we're not finished yet. No, no, no – not yet. Go outside and score one more, two more, because after that the game is dead.' But we allowed Liverpool to play for ten minutes – only ten minutes out of 120 – and that cost us the game.

Carlo's only mistake? He didn't choose me to take a penalty. In the final in Manchester, against Juventus, I took a penalty and scored. In Istanbul, Carlo didn't pick me, and this is his only mistake with me in eight years together. Not bad, eh?

CONCLUSION

CHRIS BRADY

Lessons from the Man

Emblazoned on the tail of Elvis Presley's private jet were the letters TCB. They stood for Taking Care of Business. If Carlo Ancelotti had such a plane, the letters would be TCP: Taking Care of People. That single epithet sums up his managerial philosophy. To repeat a quote by Pat Summitt, 'People don't care how much you know until they know how much you care.' Similarly, when Fabio Capello advised David Beckham to join Milan on loan, he told him, 'Carlo will take care of you.'

Taking care of people is not something that can be learned in the traditional sense. It is a quality that is acquired informally from childhood observations and a natural empathy. Carlo is genuinely patient, almost to the point of stoicism, and he admits that he can hang on to that patience too long at times. He has a serenity in a business of almost perpetual intensity, which enables him to transfer his calmness to others; this is the essence of his 'quiet' approach.

Carlo does not have to affect authenticity. He is willing to take the time to listen to anybody, irrespective of their rank or any lack of accepted knowledge about his beloved game, in the understanding that ignoring them may mean that they won't come again with what might be a key piece of information. He values relationship building above all things in his leadership roles and his method is built on influencing rather than cajoling or demanding.

Above all, Carlo Ancelotti believes in the centrality of the 'family' in everything he does. For him, being able to trust colleagues in the same way he would his own family is an essential ingredient for success. If that family feel does not exist within a club when he arrives, he will create it within the area in which he has control – with the players and his staff. A key part of the 'quiet' philosophy is not to worry about the things over which you have no control.

There needs to be a distance between the leader and the follower. Carlo sees no difficulty or contradiction in maintaining both the closeness of the relationship and the professionalism of distance. We may all be in the family and love each other, he argues, but there is still a father, a mother, an older sibling, with separate roles to play in the running of the family. As long as everybody knows that the family comes first, they will respect the roles and decisions made by the leader.

It is hard to become accepted as a member of what he calls his 'football family', but it is equally hard to be excluded, once admitted. The interviews in this book are evidence of the enduring bond he creates between himself and those with whom he works.

As Carlo mentioned earlier in the book, he is a believer in Peter Drucker's famous saying, whether apocryphal or not: 'Culture eats strategy for breakfast.' Cultural fit is, therefore, essential to Carlo's managerial philosophy. In a recent *Harvard Business Review* article, Boris Groysberg and Abhijit Naik referenced some compelling research carried out in the 1990s by Jeff Borland and Jeanette Ngaire Lye.* That research concluded that cultural fit really does matter; it is not a 'nice to have' add-on, but is essential to peak performance.

Seven coaches lost their jobs in the NFL on 2015's Black Monday, the first day after the end of the regular season when head coaches who have failed to meet the owners' expectations are traditionally fired. All the resulting vacancies were filled in less than a month. How much due diligence took place with

* Jeff Borland and Jenny Lye, 'Matching and Mobility in the Market for Australian Rules Football Coaches', *Industrial and Labor Relations Review*, October 1996; see http://hbswk.hbs.edu/item/super-bowl-coaches-how-well-do-they-fit-their-teams.

regard to cultural fit on both sides of those deals? Although we know that cultural fit matters, we still only give it the most cursory attention. As Groysberg and Naik point out, 'the processes used to determine a good fit are deemed successful after the fact – a classic case of survival bias'. There is no such thing as a pleasant surprise when taking on a new job. Even with his ill-fated sojourn at Juventus, Carlo knew precisely what he had taken on. He made his decision in full knowledge of the cultural challenge he would have to face.

Once into any business, irrespective of whether you find some unexpected surprises, you are responsible for the culture that you oversee. A 'winning mentality' is an essential element of the cultural environment for Carlo. Alessandro Nesta, for example, explained how Ancelotti was very explicit about the nature of the Milan philosophy, where winning was not an optional extra, but a necessity.

All the people interviewed for this book said that his obsession with winning permeated everything that went on within their clubs. Indeed, they said that it was a common theme among all of the big managers for whom they had played, and Carlo himself mentioned it when talking about the managers he respected both from his playing days and in his current management career.

Talent Management

Once the culture is embedded, due attention needs to be given to the actual business itself. The product in football is, very simply, what happens on the pitch. Without a quality product (a winning team), the other revenue streams are adversely affected. This is the area where the Ancelotti model is at its most relevant. At the level at which he now operates, managing the highly paid talent is a central responsibility. Bayern Munich chief executive Karl-Heinz Rummenigge has said: 'Carlo Ancelotti has enjoyed success as a coach everywhere he has been and has won the Champions League three times. Carlo is a quiet, balanced professional who knows how to deal with stars and play a game with a lot of variety. That is what we were looking for and that is what we found.'

It does seem to be a good fit at Bayern. As at all the European 'super clubs' the ultimate prize will be the Champions League. It is not surprising, therefore, that they chose the coach with the highest number of Champions League victories to his name. As such, the pressure to win the trophy again will not faze Ancelotti – after all, he delivered 'La Décima' to Madrid after a twelve-year drought in his first season.

The management of the talent becomes the key element of the job description at the highest level. Although the organization now takes responsibility for the search, acquisition and disposal elements of the talent cycle, the manager still has the responsibility to utilize those assets in the most effective way. It is the manager who has to take responsibility for the development and retention elements of the cycle. Ancelotti has had to address both the realities and the myths of the talent economy.

Many of the myths propagated by talent-management 'experts' have been successfully challenged by Dana Minbaeva and David Collings.* Among them are myths with which my fellow collaborator Mike Forde is very familiar. Mike spent five years as Chelsea's director of football operations and now consults with high-performance sports teams including the NBA's San Antonio Spurs, coached by Gregg Popovich. He argues that the realities of talent management are actually straightforward but sometimes counter-intuitive.

One such myth is that it's all about the people. The war-for-talent ethos was premised on getting the talent in and believing that the performances would take care of themselves. Wrong! Talent needs and wants direction – that's called management. Another myth was that filling all positions with 'A'

---

* Dana Minbaeva and David Collings, 'Seven Myths of Global Talent Management', *International Journal of Human Resource Management* 24, 9 (2013).

players guaranteed success. Pérez's *galácticos* policy at Madrid has pretty much undermined that theory.

The next myth that Minbaeva and Collings exposed is that talent turnover is always bad for the organization. Stability is king, goes the myth. Not so, says Mike Forde, who argues that organizations should simply accept that the talent will leave. Few highly talented people are looking for a job for life. Indeed, the average graduate changes jobs eleven times in their career; the average elite footballer 3.8 times. And that's in a career that probably lasts less than ten years. Organizations need to understand that the talent chooses them, not the other way round. The new reality is that leaders should be seeking productivity in the present, not loyalty for the future. All football managers understand this, and Carlo is no different.

Perhaps one of the most dangerous myths is that talent is portable. Talent is, in fact, very culturally dependent. Onboarding talent into any organization is difficult enough without the added complications of acclimatizing to a new language and culture. Carlo identifies learning the language as a key component of cultural integration, which is, in turn, essential to success.

Mike Forde explains that what Carlo does intuitively is recognize the talent realities. Big talent comes with big ego; accept it and manage it, that's your job. Recruit the big egos who have, in

Gregg Popovich's terms, 'got over themselves'. In other words, they've grown up. They will be priced for value. Reserve the most praise for the foot soldiers. Consult the talent – they welcome it and they add value. Influence, don't command. As Ancelotti says: 'Don't demotivate; our job is to motivate them by providing the challenges and goals their talent demands.' Develop the talent; great leaders create a learning culture and a willingness to challenge the status quo.

Finally, gauge the moment when a talent reaches its peak. As Arsène Wenger puts it, 'Buy at the bottom of the market; sell at the top. Simple economics.'

Carlo Ancelotti has naturally confronted both the myths and realities of the talent-management dilemma without reference to complex management theories. He has learned on the job and has earned the right to be called a leadership guru. He is able to accept the realities of modern leadership in any sector, be it business or sport. We spoke earlier in this book about a natural leadership arc. Pep Guardiola, for example, has argued that the arc's natural length is about three years, and some of Carlo's arcs at his clubs back this up to some degree, but we think this is too prescriptive and amounts to a planned redundancy model. That is, of course, not unknown in what has become another modern spectator sport – the financial services industry. Carlo works on the basis that he will be at his club for ever, while simultaneously understanding that it could end tomorrow.

Writing in *The Times*, sports journalist of the year and former number one British table tennis player Matthew Syed asks us to imagine which modern football managers would succeed in different contexts – at, say, a great business or charity. 'These are the leaders who understand human nature,' he writes, 'and, by implication, how to create a sustainable, enriching culture.' He might have been describing Carlo Ancelotti. In that elite echelon of modern-day managers – Sir Alex Ferguson, Pep Guardiola, José Mourinho and Arsène Wenger – Ancelotti still stands out for his uniquely quiet style.

He certainly does not 'napalm the native culture before moving on', a habit Syed memorably attributes to Mourinho. Instead, Ancelotti seduces the native culture, and when he moves on, that culture remains not only intact, but enriched for his intervention. Leave the club, team, business or organization in better shape than when you found it: that's surely the most anyone can ask.

QUIET LEADERSHIP: THE RESULTS

ANCELOTTI, THE PLAYER

Roma

- European Cup runner-up: 1983–84
- Serie A winner: 1982–83
- Coppa Italia winner: 1979–80, 1980–81, 1983–84, 1985–86

Milan

- European Cup winner: 1988–89, 1989–90
- Serie A winner: 1987–88, 1991–92
- UEFA Super Cup winner: 1989, 1990
- Supercoppa Italiana winner: 1988
- Intercontinental Cup winner: 1989, 1990

ANCELOTTI, THE ASSISTANT MANAGER

- World Cup runners-up: 1994

ANCELOTTI, THE MANAGER

Reggiana
- Serie B fourth place (winning promotion to Serie A): 1995–96

Parma
- Serie A runners-up: 1996–97

Juventus
- Serie A runners-up: 1999–2000, 2000–01
- UEFA Intertoto Cup winners: 1999

Milan
- UEFA Champions League winners: 2002–03, 2006–07
- Serie A winners: 2003–04
- UEFA Super Cup winners: 2003, 2007
- FIFA Club World Cup winners: 2007
- Coppa Italia winners: 2002–03
- Supercoppa Italiana winners: 2004

Chelsea
- Premier League winners: 2009–10
- FA Cup winners: 2009–10
- FA Community Shield winners: 2009

Paris Saint-Germain

- Ligue 1 winners: 2012–13

Real Madrid

- UEFA Champions League winners: 2013–14
- UEFA Super Cup winners: 2014
- FIFA Club World Cup winners: 2014
- Copa del Rey winners: 2013–14

INDIVIDUAL AWARDS

- Serie A Coach of the Year: 2001, 2004
- Ligue 1 Manager of the Year: 2012–13
- UEFA Manager of the Year: 2002–03
- Italian Football Hall of Fame: 2014

Acknowledgements

From Carlo

First must come the people who helped most with the book, my wife Mariann and my friends, Chris and Mike. I must also thank Ibra, Cristiano, JT, David, Paulo, Alessandro, Roberto, Sr Galliani, Sir Alex and Paul for giving up their time to be interviewed.

From Chris:

Carlo – for being the footballer, the coach but mostly, the man I wished I could have been.

Mariann – for her enduring patience with my constant badgering and being the perfect hostess when we invaded her home for access to her husband.

Maria Tawn – for her tremendous patience in making the whole venture possible by transcribing the endless hours of interviews.

Daniela and Bebe Domini – for firstly enabling the Adriano Galliani interview, secondly conducting the interview and finally for looking after us so well.

Dave and Sarah from Chez Fred – for caring enough to ask how it was going no matter how busy they were.

Starbucks in Surfside, Florida – for letting me sit all day writing with just one coffee.

From Mike

Carlo – for his patience and passion to share his ideas and for his friendship which hasn't waivered over the many years I have had the privilege of learning from him.

Mariann – for being the rock that held us all together and keeping the important messages front and centre throughout the process.

Chris – for his tremendous energy and enthusiasm for the subject and for being the best example of 'getting it done' I have ever seen.

Kevin Roberts – for showing me what leading great talent really entailed, especially early in my career when every young man needs a role model.